THE
HOLIDAY TABLE
CUISINE & CRAFTS

Cooking Club
of
America®

Minnetonka, Minnesota

THE HOLIDAY TABLE
CUISINE & CRAFTS

1 2 3 4 5 6 7 8 / 08 07 06 05 04 03

ISBN 1-58159-213-2

Cooking Club of America
12301 Whitewater Drive
Minnetonka, MN 55343
www.cookingclub.com

Tom Carpenter
Creative Director

Heather Koshiol
Managing Editor

Jennifer Guinea
Senior Book Development Coordinator

Jenya Prosmitsky
Book Design

Laura Holle
Assistant Book Development Coordinator

Mark Macemon
Commissioned Photography

Mary Evans
Michele Anna Jordan
Kathleen Prisant
Mark Scarbrough
Bruce Weinstein
Recipe Developers

Yula Nelson
Craft Developer and Stylist

Susan Brosious
Food Stylist

Jerry Dudycha
Assistant Food Stylist

Michele Joy
Prop Stylist

Special thanks to: Marcia Brinkley, Terry Casey, Janice Cauley, Cindy Jurgensen, John Laurenstein, Nancy Maurer, Mary Jo Myers and Ruth Petran.

On the Cover: Mendiant, page 182.
On Page 1: Roasted Chicken with Olive-Polenta Stuffing, page 118.

This book's title, THE HOLIDAY TABLE, *could make you think that all its ideas are related to Christmas. Let's dispel that notion right away!*

To all of us here at the Cooking Club of America, the entire year is full of holidays. Spring, summer, fall and winter ... reasons to celebrate abound. There's no sound reason to limit good food and good cheer in your life!

Sometimes the occasions are traditional — Thanksgiving, Christmas, New Year's and Easter come to mind. Sometimes the occasions make the calendar, but they aren't on everyone's "must celebrate" list — Valentine's Day, Memorial Day and the Fourth of July for instance. But many other occasions (birthdays, anniversaries and other important life milestones) fit the idea of what a holiday is too, and are certainly made for celebrating with family and friends.

No matter what the holiday, there's one place everyone gathers to commemorate and honor the occasion: the table. It's where we go to talk, visit, relax, reconnect, recollect, laugh ... and of course share good food.

That's where *The Holiday Table* comes in. This collection of *Cuisine & Crafts* will help you make your holiday table a taste-filled and attractive place to be, a showcase that you will be proud of and that your guests will remember for a long time.

So here is awesome cuisine in the form of 100 incredible recipes — many pictured in full color — that you can pick and choose from to make your own wonderful holiday meals. You'll also find 20 easy-to-create hand crafts (complete with step-by-step photo instructions) that will make your holiday table warm, friendly and inviting.

Remember. Traditional holidays are good. But a year is too long and life is too short to wait for them. So add some more holidays to your life ... and make sure your holiday table is filled with attention-getting cuisine and crafts every time.

Spring HOLIDAYS

TINY JOHNNY CAKES WITH SMOKED SALMON

Small cornmeal griddlecakes topped with silky smoked salmon whet morning appetites. Serve these cakes to your guests with orange juice or mimosas (a mixture of Champagne and orange juice) before sitting down to brunch.

½	cup sour cream
1	tablespoon grated onion
1	tablespoon minced fresh dill
½	cup water
¼	teaspoon salt
½	cup cornmeal
1	tablespoon butter
¾	cup plus 2 tablespoons milk
2	oz. smoked salmon, cut into thin strips
6	sprigs fresh dill

6 servings.
Preparation time: 40 minutes.
Ready to serve: 40 minutes.

1 In small bowl, mix sour cream, onion and dill. Cover and refrigerate.

2 In heavy medium saucepan, bring water to a boil; stir in salt. While whisking, add cornmeal in slow, steady stream. Cook, stirring constantly, about 1 minute. Using whisk, stir in butter and milk to create batter.

3 Heat griddle or large skillet; brush lightly with butter. Drop batter, one tablespoon at a time, onto griddle. Cook over low heat until golden on bottom, about 1 minute. Turn and cook until second side is golden. Keep warm in oven until all cakes are cooked.

4 For each serving, arrange three johnnycakes on small plate. Top with sour cream sauce and strips of smoked salmon. Garnish each with sprig of dill.

CHEESE THINS WITH HERBED CREAM CHEESE SPREAD

These crackers are like crisp little cookies, but they're made with Parmesan cheese instead of sugar. Make these crackers up to 2 days ahead and store in an airtight container. You can make the Cream Cheese Spread 1 to 2 days ahead and refrigerate.

CHEESE THINS

2	cups all-purpose flour
¼	teaspoon salt
½	cup butter, cut into ½-inch pieces
1½	cups (6 oz.) shredded Parmesan cheese
1	egg yolk
½	cup ice water

CREAM CHEESE SPREAD

1	(8-oz.) pkg. cream cheese, softened
2	tablespoons butter, softened
1	tablespoon minced fresh oregano
½	teaspoon minced fresh sage
⅛	teaspoon ground cumin
⅛	teaspoon salt

6 servings.
Preparation time: 35 minutes.
Ready to serve: 60 minutes.

1 Heat oven to 350°F.

2 For Cheese: In large bowl, mix flour and salt. Using pastry blender, cut in butter until mixture resembles coarse cornmeal. Stir in cheese. Mix egg yolk with ¼ cup of the water; stir into flour mixture. If necessary, add the remaining water, 1 tablespoon at a time. Gather dough into ball; divide evenly into two balls.

3 On lightly floured surface, roll dough to ³⁄₁₆ inch thick. Cut out crackers using 2-inch round biscuit cutter. Arrange crackers on baking sheets; prick each with fork. Bake 10 minutes or until golden. Carefully turn and bake an additional 10 to 15 minutes or until golden. Crackers will crisp as they cool.

4 For Cheese Spread: In small bowl, blend together cream cheese, butter, oregano, sage, cumin and salt. Cover and refrigerate until ready to serve.

ROASTED TOMATO SOUP

Fresh garden vegetables need very little cooking to celebrate their bright flavors. Roasting the tomatoes caramelizes them, adding sweetness. After they've cooled, it's easy to pull off the tomato skins before adding the pulp to the simmered vegetables.

SOUP

3	lb. ripe tomatoes
3	tablespoons olive oil
1	sweet onion, cut into thin, matchstick-size strips
1	small bulb fennel, white part only, cut into thin, matchstick-size strips
1	large carrot, peeled, cut into thin, matchstick-size strips
4	cups vegetable or chicken stock
6	sprigs fresh oregano
6	sprigs fresh thyme
4	sprigs fresh parsley
½	cup heavy cream (optional)
¾	cup (3 oz.) crumbled goat cheese

FRIED SHALLOTS

3	shallots, peeled
1	cup peanut oil or vegetable oil
1	teaspoon salt

8 servings.
Preparation time: 45 minutes.
Ready to serve: 1 hour.

1 Heat oven to 450°F. Cut tomatoes in half. Remove seeds by gently squeezing tomatoes over small bowl. Strain and reserve juices.

2 For Soup: Arrange tomatoes, cut-side down, on jelly-roll pan; drizzle with 1 tablespoon of olive oil. Bake 30 minutes. Remove from oven; cool. Discard skin; reserve pulp and juices.

3 In heavy, large saucepan, heat remaining 2 tablespoons olive oil over medium heat until hot. Add onion, fennel and carrot; sauté until soft, about 10 minutes. Add stock. Tie oregano, thyme and parsley together with kitchen string; add to saucepan. Heat to a boil, then reduce heat to low; simmer 20 minutes. Remove herbs. Add tomatoes and juices; heat until hot. If desired, stir in cream; heat until warm, do not boil.

4 For Shallots: Cut shallots into paper-thin slices and separate rings. Soak in ice water 10 minutes; drain and pat dry. Cover plate with several layers of paper towels. In large saucepan, heat oil over medium-high heat until hot. In batches, add shallot slices; cook until crisp, turning as necessary, about 6 to 8 minutes. Using mesh strainer or slotted spoon, remove shallots to paper towels. Sprinkle with salt.

5 Top each serving evenly with 2 tablespoons goat cheese and 1 to 2 tablespoons fried shallots.

SEAFOOD APPETIZER

This is a version of ceviche, a classic appetizer served in many of Mexico's seaside resorts. Tender filet of sole is poached just until cooked through and then gently mixed with brightly seasoned tomatoes and lime juice. Serve Seafood Appetizer *with lots of chips.*

1	cup water
½	cup plus 2 tablespoons fresh lime juice
1	(1-1b.) sole filet, cut into ½-inch squares
1	tomato, seeded and diced
⅓	cup minced red onion
¼	cup minced parsley
2	tablespoons olive oil
½	teaspoon hot pepper sauce, or to taste
½	teaspoon salt
1	slightly firm avocado, cut into ½-inch cubes
1	quart tortilla chips

6 (½-cup) servings.
Preparation time: 30 minutes.
Ready to serve: 1 hour, 30 minutes.

1 In large skillet, mix water and ½ cup of the lime juice; bring to a boil. Add fish, cover and simmer 2 to 3 minutes or until cooked through. Drain.

2 In serving bowl; mix tomato, onion, parsley, olive oil, remaining 2 tablespoons lime juice, hot pepper sauce and salt. Gently stir in fish and avocado. Cover and refrigerate until cold, about 1 hour.

3 Taste and add more hot sauce, if desired. Arrange in center of platter with chips around edge.

TIP* This dish is delicious when heated and served as a filling for fish tacos.

DECOUPAGE COASTERS

Create beautiful personalized decoupage coasters. This set celebrates the blooming of the beloved cherry blossom tree. Decoupage is easy and fun to do. Try a variation by using your child's artwork. You will both enjoy creating a personal set of coasters for the kids to use.

DIRECTIONS

1 Trace the coaster onto plain paper. Then trace it onto the decorative paper. Cut the circles.

2 Brush decoupage medium onto the back side of the plain paper and place it on top of the coaster. This layer prevents the cork coaster from showing through the decorative paper. Let it dry.

3 Brush decoupage medium onto the back side of the decorative paper and apply it to the coaster. After it has dried, cut off any excess paper using scissors. Spray several coatings of clear acrylic spray sealant. This will protect the paper from water. Applying gold metallic marker to the edge of the coasters is optional.

MINI PIZZA PRIMAVERA

Create a hit at your backyard barbecue with these little pizzas. This vegetable topping is just a suggestion. Sauté any of your favorite vegetables and add your own choice of cheese. If kids are on the scene, set out kid-friendly toppings of black, pitted olives, shredded cheddar cheese and cherry tomatoes.

2	tablespoons olive oil
1	zucchini, chopped
1	Japanese eggplant, chopped
1	yellow onion, chopped
2	garlic cloves, finely chopped
½	teaspoon salt
½	teaspoon freshly ground pepper
1	pint cherry tomatoes, cut into quarters
2	cups baby spinach leaves
3	tablespoons chopped fresh basil
1	lb. frozen bread dough, thawed
2	tablespoons olive oil
1	cup (4 oz.) crumbled Gorgonzola cheese

6 servings.
Preparation time: 30 minutes.
Ready to serve: 40 minutes.

1 In large skillet, heat 2 tablespoons olive oil over medium heat. Add zucchini, eggplant, onion and garlic; cook, stirring occasionally until tender, about 5 minutes. Add salt, pepper, cherry tomatoes, spinach and basil; cook until spinach is wilted, about 1 to 2 minutes. Reserve vegetable mixture.

2 Heat grill to medium. Cut dough into six pieces. Roll and stretch dough to form 6 (6-inch) circles. Brush top of each circle with olive oil. Place on grill, oiled-side down. Cook 3 minutes or until bottom of crusts are browned; turn. Top each crust with ½ cup each reserved vegetable mixture, sprinkle each with about 2 tablespoons cheese.

3 Grill until bottoms of crusts are golden and slightly crisp and cheese has melted, about 5 minutes. Serve immediately.

RED AND GREEN CABBAGE SLAW

This salad has a clean flavor and crisp texture. You may choose to serve it as an accompaniment to the Roasted Chiles Rellenos *(page 29) and* Seasoned Black Beans and Warm Tortillas *(page 35).*

3	cups shredded red cabbage, rinsed, dried
3	cups shredded green cabbage, rinsed, dried
¼	cup chopped fresh mint
2	tablespoons seasoned rice vinegar
1	tablespoon fresh lime juice
1	teaspoon cumin seeds, toasted
½	teaspoon salt
¼	teaspoon freshly ground pepper
2	tablespoons olive oil

1 In large bowl, combine red and green cabbage and mint.

2 In small bowl, combine rice vinegar, lime juice, cumin seeds, salt and pepper. Whisk in olive oil. Drizzle over cabbage mixture; toss. (Salad can be prepared up to 12 hours ahead.) Cover and refrigerate. Bring to room temperature before serving.

6 servings.
Preparation time: 10 minutes.
Ready to serve: 10 minutes.

SALAD OF BABY ARUGULA WITH PAPER-THIN JICAMA

Lemon and honey taste wonderful with the crisp, green apple flavor of jicama. If jicama is not available, use tart green apples instead.

1	tablespoon lemon peel
2	tablespoons fresh lemon juice
1	tablespoon honey
½	teaspoon salt
¼	teaspoon freshly ground pepper
1	tablespoon extra-virgin olive oil
¼	lb. jicama, peeled
6	cups baby arugula leaves

1 In small bowl, mix lemon peel, juice, honey, salt and pepper. Whisk in olive oil.

2 Using a vegetable peeler or sharp knife, cut jicama into paper-thin slices; toss with dressing.

3 Arrange arugula evenly on 6 salad plates. Divide jicama evenly between salad plates; drizzle with dressing.

6 servings.
Preparation time: 15 minutes.
Ready to serve: 17 minutes.

WATERCRESS SALAD WITH CUCUMBER AND RED ONION

This simple Watercress Salad with Cucumber and Red Onion *is wonderfully refreshing when served between courses or with the entree.*

2	bunches watercress
1	cucumber, peeled, seeded, cut into thin, matchstick-size strips
¼	red onion, thinly sliced
2	tablespoons white wine vinegar
⅛	teaspoon salt
	Pinch ground white pepper
⅓	cup extra-virgin olive oil

6 (1-cup) servings.
Preparation time: 15 minutes.
Ready to serve: 15 minutes.

1 Trim larger stems from watercress. Wash and dry. In large salad bowl, toss watercress, cucumber and red onion.

2 In medium bowl, blend vinegar, salt and pepper with whisk until salt has dissolved. Whisk in olive oil. Just before serving, toss dressing with watercress mixture.

CHOPPED SALAD WITH RANCH DRESSING

You can use low-fat buttermilk and low-fat mayonnaise to turn this into a terrific salad for calorie-watchers.

¾   cup buttermilk

½   cup mayonnaise

2   tablespoons chopped chives or green onion

1   garlic clove, minced

¼   teaspoon salt

¼   teaspoon freshly ground pepper

1   small head romaine lettuce, washed,
         chopped into 1-inch pieces

1   green bell pepper, chopped

1   red bell pepper, chopped

1   large tomato, seeded, chopped

1   large carrot, peeled, chopped

1   slightly firm avocado, peeled, cut into
         ½-inch cubes

6 servings.
Preparation time: 30 minutes.
Ready to serve: 30 minutes.

1 In small bowl, combine buttermilk, mayonnaise, chives, garlic, salt and pepper. Cover and refrigerate 30 minutes to allow flavors to blend.

2 In large salad bowl, toss lettuce, bell peppers, tomato, carrot and avocado. Add dressing; toss again.

This is a simply elegant way to embellish a napkin. Brighten up each person's place setting with an exquisite fresh flower. The fragrant flower also becomes a gift for your guests to enjoy. Try using dahlias for a summertime variation.

MATERIALS AND TOOLS

❑ PEONIES
❑ NAPKINS
❑ RIBBON
❑ FLORAL WATER TUBES
❑ SCISSORS

DIRECTIONS

1 Fold the top and bottom of the napkin to the center.

2 Fold the bottom above where the two ends meet, creating a pocket for the flower.

3 Fold the napkin in half and then fold it in thirds. Tie a bow around the bottom half of the folded napkin. Insert the cut flower into a water-filled tube and place it inside the pocket of the folded napkin.

Spring Beet Salad

Cooking beets in heavily salted water helps keep the color from bleeding. If salt is a concern, replace it with about ¼ cup of white wine vinegar.

1	lb. mixed yellow and red baby beets (about 8 baby beets or 4 larger beets)
2	tablespoons white wine vinegar
1	teaspoon grated orange peel
1	teaspoon freshly snipped tarragon
½	teaspoon salt
¼	teaspoon freshly ground pepper
2	tablespoons olive oil
1	firm avocado, peeled, diced
2	cups mixed spring greens

6 servings.
Preparation time: 20 minutes.
Ready to serve: 25 minutes.

1 Trim greens and roots from beets; wash well. Cut beets into ½-inch cubes. Cook two colors of beets separately in heavily salted* boiling water until tender, about 8 minutes; drain.

2 In medium bowl, combine vinegar, orange peel, tarragon, salt and pepper; mix well. Drizzle each color of beets with half of the vinegar mixture; let sit 10 minutes. Stir half of the oil into each color of beets.

3 Using slotted spoon, combine beets in one large bowl. Stir in avocado. Arrange small pile of beets evenly on each salad plate. Surround with small ring of mixed greens. Drizzle greens evenly with dressing from the beets.

TIP* "Heavily salted water" is 1 tablespoon of salt to about 1 quart of water.

BRINED AND GRILLED CORNISH GAME HENS

Because of their petite size, game hens can easily dry out when you cook them. A preliminary bath in salty water preserves the moisture in these little birds. Poultry seasoning is a packaged mixture of marjoram, sage, thyme and other herbs that vary by brand. Read labels and choose the mixture that sounds most delicious to you ... or buy some spices (such as those mentioned above) and make your own!

3	(1½-lb.) Cornish game hens, cut into halves
3	quarts water
1½	cups kosher (coarse) salt
¼	cup sugar
¼	cup poultry seasoning

6 servings.

Preparation time: 15 minutes.
Ready to serve: 2 hours, 30 minutes.

1 Place halved game hens in large bowl. Mix water, salt and sugar; pour over game hens. Cover and refrigerate at least 1½ hours or overnight.

2 Heat grill. Remove hens from water mixture; pat dry. Sprinkle poultry seasoning over hens, rub into skin.

3 Place hens on gas grill over medium-low heat, or on charcoal grill 4 to 6 inches from medium coals. Grill, turning occasionally, about 20 to 25 minutes or until juices run clear when thickest part is pricked with a fork.

POACHED TUNA WITH SHAVED FENNEL AND RED ONION

Lightly poached seafood creates a perfect transition to springtime dining. Tuna is a treat, but any firm fish can be substituted. Star anise, often used in Asian recipes, is a fragrant spice worthy of keeping on hand. It is available in whole stars or powdered.

1	quart water
1	cup dry white wine
6	whole peppercorns, cracked
2	buds star anise
	Peel from 1 lemon
1	teaspoon salt
6	(6-oz.) pieces fresh tuna or other firm-fleshed fish
1	small bulb fennel, cut into paper-thin slices
1	small red onion, cut into paper-thin slices
3	tablespoons cold butter, cut into 6 pieces
2	tablespoons snipped chervil or chives

6 servings.
Preparation time: 15 minutes.
Ready to serve: 45 minutes.

1 In large sauté pan, mix water, wine, peppercorns, star anise, lemon peel and salt. Bring mixture to a boil over medium-high heat. Add tuna steaks; reduce heat to a gentle simmer. Cover and simmer 5 to 10 minutes or until tuna flakes easily with a fork. Remove tuna to warm platter; cover and keep warm.

2 Strain poaching liquid; return to skillet. Add fennel and red onion slices. Simmer over high heat until vegetables are tender, about 5 minutes. Remove vegetables to tuna platter; cover and keep warm.

3 Continue cooking poaching liquid until reduced to about 1 cup. Whisk in butter, one piece at a time. Arrange fennel and red onion on each dinner plate, top with tuna steak. Drizzle with sauce. Sprinkle each serving with chervil or chives.

SOUFFLED OMELET ROLL WITH SWEET PEPPER SAUCE

This Easter Brunch entrée calls for a formal presentation. Place the omelet on a platter and drizzle it with the bright red pepper sauce before cutting it into slices.

OMELET

½	cup all-purpose flour
2	cups milk
6	eggs, separated
¼	teaspoon salt
⅛	teaspoon ground white pepper
⅛	teaspoon freshly ground nutmeg
½	cup (2 oz.) shredded Gruyère or Swiss cheese

FILLING

1	tablespoon olive oil
2	shallots, minced (about ⅓ cup)
1	lb. baby spinach leaves, washed, dried
¼	teaspoon salt
¼	teaspoon ground white pepper
½	teaspoon white wine vinegar

SWEET PEPPER SAUCE

1	(15-oz.) jar roasted red bell peppers, rinsed, drained
1	garlic clove, chopped
2	tablespoons chopped fresh oregano
2	teaspoons fresh lemon juice
½	teaspoon salt
½	teaspoon sugar
⅓	cup olive oil

6 servings.
Preparation time: 25 minutes.
Ready to serve: 45 minutes.

1 Heat oven to 375°F. Line jelly-roll pan with aluminum foil or parchment paper.

2 For Omelet: Place flour in heavy medium saucepan. Using whisk, stir in just enough milk to make smooth paste. Stir in remaining milk until smooth. Cook over medium heat, stirring constantly, until thickened, about 3 minutes. Remove from heat. Beat in egg yolks, one at a time. Whisk in salt, pepper and nutmeg. Stir in cheese. Beat egg whites until stiff but not dry. Fold about 1 cup of the egg whites into the yolk mixture. Gently fold in remaining whites. Spread into prepared pan. Bake 18 to 20 minutes or until puffed and light brown. Gently lift soufflé from pan using edges of the paper; turn over onto large platter. Gently run knife under paper to remove.

3 For Filling: In large skillet, heat oil over medium heat until hot. Add shallots, cook until softened but not browned, about 3 minutes. Add spinach, salt and pepper; cook and stir until spinach is wilted; stir in vinegar. Place in colander over bowl. Let sit, covered, until ready to use.

4 For Sauce: In blender or food processor, combine peppers, garlic, oregano, lemon juice, salt and sugar; cover and blend until smooth. With blender running, add oil in slow, steady stream. In small saucepan, heat sauce over medium heat before serving. (Sauce can be prepared up to 24 hours ahead. Cover and refrigerate.)

5 Spread soufflé evenly with filling. Using a wide spatula, roll omelet starting at long end. Drizzle with some of sauce. Serve remaining sauce separately.

ROASTED CHILES RELLENOS

These rellenos are not fried, but simply roasted, peeled and filled with a creamy chicken filling. You can prepare the chicken mixture and peppers up to 8 hours in advance and refrigerate. When ready to serve, fill the peppers and bake until they're hot. If you have leftover stock, freeze it for another use.

7	large poblano chiles (sometimes called pasilla chiles)
1	½ lb. boneless, skinless chicken breasts
2	cups chicken broth
1	cup water
1	tablespoon chopped fresh oregano
1	bay leaf
1	teaspoon cumin
½	teaspoon cinnamon
¼	teaspoon salt
3	tablespoons butter
3	tablespoons all-purpose flour
1	cup (4 oz.) shredded Monterey Jack or cheddar cheese
1	cup sour cream
	Paprika for garnish

6 servings.
Preparation time: 45 minutes.
Ready to serve: 1 hour.

1 Heat grill to medium-high heat or broiler. Cook chiles 4 to 6 inches from heat, about 8 to 10 minutes, turning occasionally, until charred on all sides. Place peppers in resealable plastic bag; let stand 5 minutes. Remove skin. Do not rinse.

2 Chop one chile; reserve. Cut slit into each of the remaining chiles from stem to tip; remove seeds. Arrange chiles in 13x9-inch glass baking dish.

3 Place chicken breasts in large saucepan. Add chicken broth, water, oregano, bay leaf, cumin, cinnamon and salt. Cover and bring to a boil; reduce heat to a very low simmer. Cook 15 minutes or until chicken is cooked through and juices run clear when cut. Remove chicken, let cool and shred. Remove and discard bay leaf.

4 Heat oven to 375°F. In medium saucepan, heat butter until melted. Add flour and cook, stirring constantly, until slightly browned, about 1 to 2 minutes. Add 2 cups of the chicken stock mixture. Cook, stirring constantly, until thickened. Stir in chicken, cheese, sour cream and chopped chile.

5 Spoon chicken mixture into each of the peppers. Sprinkle each with paprika. Bake until heated through, about 10 to 15 minutes.

SMOKED CHICKEN RAVIOLI WITH HERBED PESTO

Luscious smoked chicken sandwiches between small wonton wrappers create quick ravioli. The ravioli can be formed and frozen to cook later. Freeze them in a single layer on baking sheets, then transfer to resealable plastic freezer bags. They'll keep in the freezer for up to a month. Cook frozen ravioli in simmering water for about 8 minutes.

1	cup fresh Italian parsley
¼	cup chopped fresh basil
2	tablespoons chopped fresh oregano
1	garlic clove, chopped
2	tablespoons shredded Asiago or Parmesan cheese
¼	teaspoon salt
⅓	cup olive oil
1	lb. smoked chicken, ground*
¼	cup heavy cream (or milk)
½	teaspoon freshly ground nutmeg
36	(4-inch square) wonton wrappers
6	large shavings Asiago or Parmesan cheese

6 servings.
Preparation time: 1 hour.
Ready to serve: 1 hour, 10 minutes.

1 In blender or food processor, combine parsley, basil, oregano, garlic, cheese and salt; cover and process until slightly smooth. With machine running, add oil in thin, steady stream; reserve. Wipe out blender or food processor.

2 Place chicken, cream and nutmeg in food processor; process until smooth. Place 4 teaspoons chicken mixture on each wonton wrapper; moisten edge of wrapper with water. Top with second wrapper; press down to seal edges. Repeat until all ravioli are filled.

3 Fill large saucepan with water. Bring to a boil over medium-high heat, then reduce heat to medium and simmer. Add ravioli in batches; cook about 4 minutes or until al dente. Using slotted spoon, remove ravioli to warm bowls. Drizzle each serving with some of the reserved herbed pesto. Top with shaving of cheese and serve immediately.

TIP* You may substitute smoked turkey.

VIOLA FLOWERPOTS

Decorate the table with potted flower gifts. Your guests will love to display these pots in their home. Also try potted herbs for a gift they can use when cooking. Experiment with pressing different herbs to decorate the pots.

MATERIALS AND TOOLS

- ❑ VIOLAS IN 4-INCH POTS (FROM LOCAL NURSERY)
- ❑ 4-INCH TERRA COTTA POTS
- ❑ SOIL MIX
- ❑ PRESSED VIOLAS AND PANSIES
- ❑ RIBBON
- ❑ DECOUPAGE MEDIUM
- ❑ WHITE ACRYLIC PAINT
- ❑ PAINTBRUSH

DIRECTIONS

1 Mix 1 cup of water with a few drops of white paint. Paint the whitewash over the pots. Add several more coats until you have reached the desired effect.

2 Gently brush decoupage medium onto the back side of a pressed flower. Place them around the pot. Allow them to dry. Apply two more coats to seal the pansies to the pot.

3 Tie a ribbon around the pot. Transfer the flowers into the pots. Add a little dirt and water.

TENDER GREEN BEANS WITH PANCETTA

This vegetable side dish is simple, but a treat. Blanch green beans and sauté them with garlic and diced bacon, then sprinkle on red pepper flakes.

1½	lb. green beans, cut into 1-inch pieces
¼	cup diced lean bacon, such as pancetta
2	garlic cloves, crushed
¼	teaspoon crushed red pepper
⅛	teaspoon salt

6 servings.
Preparation time: 10 minutes.
Ready to serve: 20 minutes.

1 Drop beans into boiling salted water. Cook until crisp tender, about 5 to 7 minutes. Drain and pat dry.

2 In large skillet, cook bacon, garlic and red pepper until bacon is slightly crisp, about 3 to 5 minutes. Add beans; cook, stirring constantly, until beans are hot. Stir in salt. Serve immediately.

FRESH LINGUINI WITH CHERRY TOMATOES, ARUGULA AND FRESH CORN

Pasta makes a great alternative to potatoes as a "feature" side dish. This easy linguini does the job with style.

1	cup sweet cherry tomatoes, quartered
1	cup corn kernels (from 2 cobs of corn)
½	teaspoon salt
1	lb. linguini
2	tablespoons olive oil
4	cups baby arugula leaves

6 servings.
Preparation time: 10 minutes.
Ready to serve: 15 minutes.

1 Heat heavy, large skillet until hot. Add tomatoes, corn and salt; cook, stirring constantly, until heated through and corn is lightly browned.

2 Meanwhile, cook linguini according to package directions; drain. Add olive oil; toss to coat. Add tomato mixture and arugula to linguini; toss well. Serve immediately.

SEASONED BLACK BEANS AND WARM TORTILLAS

Beans are a staple with Mexican meals. Canned beans are quick to heat and can be easily dressed up with fresh herbs and toppings. To accompany Roasted Chiles Rellenos *(page 129), sprinkle the beans with fresh lime juice, diced red onion and Mexican queso anejo or dry Jack cheese.*

2	(15-oz.) cans black beans, drained, rinsed
2	tablespoons chopped fresh oregano
1	bay leaf
⅓	cup diced red onion
⅓	cup crumbled Mexican cheese, such as queso anejo or grated dry Jack cheese
1	lime, cut into 6 wedges
12	small flour tortillas, warmed*

6 servings.
Preparation time: 15 minutes.
Ready to serve: 25 minutes.

1 In medium saucepan, mix beans, oregano and bay leaf. Simmer over very low heat 10 minutes or until hot, stirring occasionally. Remove and discard bay leaf.

2 Top each serving with onion and cheese. Serve with a wedge of lime and warm tortillas.

TIP* To warm tortillas, wrap in aluminum foil and heat in 300°F oven 10 minutes or until warm. Serve wrapped in a clean dish towel or linen cloth napkin.

COUNTRY BREAD WITH SWEET AND SAVORY SPREAD

Instead of plain butter on toast, try this simple mixture of sweet preserves and savory goat cheese. To serve toast for a group, arrange several slices of bread on a broiler pan and toast them all at once, but watch them carefully because the broiler will toast the bread very quickly!

1	(about 1-lb.) loaf crusty country-style bread, cut into 1-inch slices
4	to 5 oz. fresh goat cheese, slightly softened
2	tablespoons butter, softened
2	tablespoons peach or apricot preserves
2	tablespoons snipped chives

6 servings.
Preparation time: 5 minutes.
Ready to serve: 8 minutes.

1 Heat broiler. In medium bowl, mix goat cheese, butter, preserves and chives.

2 Arrange bread slices on baking sheet; broil until golden. If desired, turn and toast bread on the opposite side.

3 Remove bread slices to serving platter; spread generously with goat cheese mixture. Serve immediately.

ROASTED SWEET PEPPER GRATIN

Flavors of the Italian countryside combine in this vegetable side dish. One idea: Serve this gratin as a base under the Brined and Grilled Cornish Hens *(page 25). The juices from the hens mingle with the sweet red peppers beautifully.*

6	red bell peppers
½	cup pitted niçoise or dry-cured ripe olives, quartered
1	cup (4 oz.) shredded mozzarella cheese
1	tablespoon dried oregano
½	teaspoon salt
2	cups bread crumbs
⅓	cup olive oil

6 servings.
Preparation time: 30 minutes.
Ready to serve: 50 minutes.

1 Heat oven to 375°F.

2 Heat grill or broiler. Cook peppers 4 to 6 inches from heat, turning occasionally, until charred on all sides, about 8 to 10 minutes. Place peppers in resealable plastic bag; let stand 5 minutes. Remove skin. Do not rinse. Cut peppers into 1-inch-square pieces.

3 In 9-inch square pan, mix peppers, olives, cheese, oregano and salt. Sprinkle with bread crumbs; drizzle with olive oil. Bake 20 to 30 minutes or until hot and bubbly.

Pussy Willow Wrapped Candle Holders

*P*ussy willows are a springtime favorite. Create a unique candle holder with organic style using pussy willow. The branches will dry beautifully attached to the candle holder, even after being freshly cut. Experiment with spray-painting branches for added pizzazz.

MATERIALS AND TOOLS

- ❏ PUSSY WILLOW BRANCHES
- ❏ CANDLE HOLDER
- ❏ VOTIVE CANDLE
- ❏ RUBBER BAND
- ❏ 2 YARDS OF VELVET RIBBON
- ❏ PRUNING SHEARS
- ❏ SCISSORS

DIRECTIONS

1 Cut the branches to a desired length using pruning shears.

2 Wrap a rubber band around the candle holder and slip the branches underneath.

3 Tie the ribbon near the bottom and cross the two ends of the ribbon twice around the front. Tie a bow at the top.

LEMON CREAM ON FRESH STRAWBERRIES

Welcome sunny weather with a big bowl of fresh strawberries topped with the bright flavor of lemony cream cheese.

1	(8-oz.) pkg. cream cheese, softened
⅓	cup sifted powdered sugar
1	tablespoon freshly grated lemon peel
3	tablespoons fresh lemon juice
2	pints strawberries, cut into halves
½	cup prepared vanilla syrup*

6 servings.
Preparation time: 15 minutes.
Ready to serve: 15 minutes.

1 In medium bowl, beat cream cheese, powdered sugar, lemon peel and lemon juice with electric mixer at medium speed until well mixed. Cover and refrigerate until serving.

2 In large bowl, toss strawberries and vanilla syrup. Cover and refrigerate until serving. Serve strawberries in bowls, topped with lemon cream.

TIP* If vanilla syrup is unavailable, heat ½ cup water and ½ cup sugar until sugar has dissolved. Stir in ½ teaspoon vanilla extract.

CHOCOLATE CREAM CHEESE MOUSSE WITH FRESH RASPBERRIES

This kid-friendly dessert is a snap to make. Light cream cheese blends deliciously with chocolate Osauce and powdered sugar. Fresh raspberries and hazelnuts dress it up.

1	(16-oz.) pkg. low-fat cream cheese, softened
¼	cup powdered sugar
¼	cup chocolate syrup
1	teaspoon vanilla extract
1	cup whipped cream or whipped topping
2	cups fresh raspberries
¼	cup chopped hazelnuts

6 servings.
Preparation time: 15 minutes.
Ready to serve: 20 minutes.

1 Using electric mixer, blend cream cheese, powdered sugar, chocolate and vanilla on medium speed until smooth. Fold in whipped cream. Divide among 6 dessert bowls. Cover and refrigerate.

2 Just before serving, top each bowl with fresh raspberries; sprinkle with hazelnuts.

GRILLED FRUIT SUNDAES

Spring is in full bloom and summer is fast approaching as the stone fruits make their appearance. Peaches, plums and apricots become tender and caramelized when they're licked with flames from the grill.

3	peaches
3	plums
6	apricots
½	teaspoon cinnamon
½	cup honey
	Vanilla ice cream or frozen yogurt
½	cup toasted, slivered almonds, if desired

6 servings.
Preparation time: 15 minutes.
Ready to serve: 25 minutes.

1 Heat grill.

2 Cut each piece of fruit into halves; remove pits*. Place in grill basket. Cook 4 to 6 inches from medium-high heat, turning fruit occasionally, until fruit is softened but not charred, about 10 minutes. Let cool slightly, then remove any charred skin. Place fruit in large serving bowl.

3 Meanwhile, mix cinnamon and honey in small microwavable bowl. Heat until honey is softened, stir into grilled fruit.

4 To serve, scoop ice cream into individual bowls. Top each serving with fruit and honey mixture. If desired, sprinkle with almonds.

TIP* If fruit pits are difficult to remove, use a grapefruit spoon or melon baller to loosen pits.

APRICOT CLOUDS

Light as a cloud and a dream to prepare, apricots and cream pair up in this sweet treat. Have all the ingredients prepared and waiting in the refrigerator until it's time for dessert. Assemble the parfaits just before serving.

9	fresh, ripe apricots*
	Sugar to taste
1½	cups cream
3	tablespoons sugar
½	teaspoon vanilla extract
1	cup biscotti or other buttery cookie crumbs
6	candied lavender petals or organic pansies, if desired

6 servings.
Preparation time: 20 minutes.
Ready to serve: 20 minutes.

1 Bring large pot of water to a boil over medium-high heat. Add apricots; boil 1 minute, then drain. Place apricots in very cold water to stop cooking and remove skins; cut each in half and remove pits.

2 Place 12 apricot halves in blender or food processor; cover and blend until smooth. If apricots are tart, add sugar to taste; blend again. Spoon mixture into medium bowl. Chop remaining apricots. Stir into pureed mixture; reserve.

3 Using electric mixer, beat cream and 3 tablespoons sugar on medium speed until softly whipped. Add vanilla extract; continue beating until slightly stiff.

4 Spoon about ¼ cup whipped cream into six wine or parfait glasses. Drizzle with 2 tablespoons apricot mixture; sprinkle with 1 tablespoon biscotti crumbs. Repeat. Top each serving with candied lavender or a fresh, organic pansy petal, if desired. Store in refrigerator.

TIP* Apricots from a can or jar work well in this recipe. Drain them before using. Use 1 (24-oz.) jar or about 1½ cans (about 16 oz. per can). You may not have to sweeten the canned apricots.

MARGARITA SORBET WITH MEXICAN WEDDING COOKIES

Sweet and puckery sour is the flavor of this easy frozen treat. It just takes a few minutes to prepare, but give it lots of time to freeze to the perfect consistency.

SORBET

1	cup sugar
1½	cups water
2	(12-oz.) cans frozen limeade concentrate, thawed
1	teaspoon orange flower water
	Grated lemon peel, for garnish

COOKIES

2	cups flour
½	cup sifted powdered sugar
1	cup almonds, finely chopped
1	cup butter, softened
¼	teaspoon almond extract
	Powdered sugar, as needed

6 servings sorbet.
Preparation time: 10 minutes.
Ready to serve: 6 to 8 hours.

36 cookies.
Preparation time: 20 minutes.
Ready to serve: 1 hour.

1 For Sorbet: In medium bowl, stir sugar and water until sugar has dissolved. Stir in limeade concentrate and orange flower water. Pour mixture into ice cream maker and freeze according to manufacturer's directions*. Spoon into freezer container; cover and freeze 6 to 8 hours or until firm. Garnish with lemon peel before serving.

2 For Cookies: Heat oven to 300°F. In large bowl, mix flour, sugar and almonds. Stir in butter and almond extract. Using floured hands, knead until the mixture forms ball. Shape into 36 (1-inch) balls. Arrange on ungreased baking sheets. Bake 25 to 30 minutes or until very lightly browned. Place on wire racks until slightly cool. Dust cookies by spooning powdered sugar through sieve held over cookies.

TIP* If an ice cream maker is not available, pour mixture into a 9-inch square, metal baking pan. Freeze about 2 hours or until mixture is frozen about 2 inches around the sides. Stir well with a fork. Repeat freezing and stirring two more times. Cover and freeze at least 1 hour before serving.

Decorate a dessert pedestal with fresh flowers from the garden to give your homemade desserts even more visual appeal. This gorgeous floral dessert pedestal was decorated with irises, ranunculus, sweet pea and Queen Anne's lace. Tulips, daffodils and other early bulbs would work well in spring. Use flowers from your local florist to create this elegant desert presentation all year round.

MATERIALS AND TOOLS

- ❏ CAKE PEDESTAL
- ❏ GLASS PLATE WITH SAME DIAMETER
- ❏ FRESH FLOWERS
- ❏ SCISSORS
- ❏ FLORIST STICKY CLAY (OPTIONAL)

DIRECTIONS

1 Cut the stems of the flowers to fit about halfway onto the surface of the pedestal.

2 Place a few flowers on top of the pedestal and put the glass plate on top the flowers.

3 Gently lifting the plate, insert the rest of the flowers around the plate. Use the sticky clay to keep the flowers in place, if necessary. Place a doily on top of the plate to cover up the cut stems, if desired.

summer HOLIDAYS

Fourth of July

Labor Day

Reunion

Birthday

Anniversary

Summer Solstice

Barbecues

Picnics

FRESH CORN ROUNDS WITH BACON-SOUR CREAM DIP

Try this sour cream dip with other vegetables too — sugar snap peas, carrots and cauliflower and other vegetables of summer would all taste great.

4	small ears young sweet corn, husked, cut into 1½-inch rounds
1	cup sour cream
4	slices cooked bacon, finely chopped
1	tablespoon powdered ranch dip mix (from 1-oz. pkg.)
1	teaspoon dried dill weed
¼	teaspoon lemon pepper

8 servings.
Preparation time: 15 minutes.
Ready to serve: 20 minutes.

1 Heat large pot of water over high heat until boiling. Add corn rounds; boil 4 minutes or until crisp tender. Drain and cool slightly.

2 In small bowl, stir together sour cream, bacon, ranch dip mix, dill weed and lemon pepper. Serve with warm or room-temperature corn rounds.

GRILLED MULTI-PEPPER CROSTINI

This simple, tasty appetizer is perfect when summer's peppers come into season. For a delightful variation, add chopped kalamata olives to the peppers.

1	red bell pepper, halved
1	orange bell pepper, halved
1	yellow bell pepper, halved
½	teaspoon minced garlic
¼	teaspoon salt
2	teaspoons lemon juice
2	tablespoons extra-virgin olive oil
1	tablespoon chopped fresh oregano
12	(½-inch-thick) slices stale French bread, cut on the diagonal

6 servings.
Preparation time: 15 minutes.
Ready to serve: 45 minutes.

1 Heat grill.

2 Place peppers, insides down, on charcoal grill 4 to 6 inches from medium coals, or on gas grill over medium heat. Cover and cook until edges are just beginning to char, about 4 to 5 minutes. Turn skin-sides down; cook, covered, until skin blackens, about 5 to 8 minutes. Remove to medium bowl; cover with plastic wrap and let cool about 15 minutes. Remove skin. Cut pepper halves into ¼-inch strips; cut strips in half crosswise. Place in clean, medium bowl.

3 On cutting board, mash garlic with salt; place in small bowl. Stir in lemon juice, olive oil and oregano. Drizzle over peppers; toss to coat. Can be made ahead and refrigerated, covered, one day in advance.

4 Grill French bread slices until browned, about 1 to 2 minutes per side. Spoon pepper mixture onto grilled bread; serve.

INDIVIDUAL PESTO PIZZAS

For variety, scatter ½ teaspoon chopped black olives, sun-dried tomatoes or roasted peppers over the pesto topping before baking making this summery pizza.

1	(7-oz.) can refrigerated breadstick dough (for 6 breadsticks)
¼	cup purchased, refrigerated pesto
¾	cup (3 oz.) shredded mozzarella or Gruyère cheese
12	basil leaves

6 servings.
Preparation time: 10 minutes.
Ready to serve: 25 minutes.

1 Heat oven to 375°F.

2 Unroll breadsticks from can; divide along perforations. Cut each breadstick in half, width-wise, to form 12 pieces. Press edges of each piece inward; pat and shape each piece into a 2½-inch circle.

3 Arrange on 17x13-inch baking sheet. Top each circle with 1 teaspoon pesto; spread to cover. Bake 12 to 14 minutes or until edges are well browned. Top each pizza with 1 tablespoon shredded mozzarella cheese; let melt slightly. Press 1 basil leaf on top of each pizza.

AVOCADO PICO DE GALLO DIP

Pico de Gallo *means rooster's beak and that's what Texans call their fresh salsa. Adding buttery, diced avocado to this popular offering gives it a fresh twist. Serve with crunchy corn chips for dipping, or use as a topping on grilled chicken or fish.*

½	cup finely chopped red onion
1½	cups finely chopped tomatoes
¼	cup chopped fresh cilantro
2	jalapeño chiles, finely chopped (seeded, if desired)
2	tablespoons lime juice
¾	teaspoon salt
2	medium ripe avocados, diced
	Corn chips

3½ cups.
Preparation time: 15 minutes.
Ready to serve: 25 minutes.

1 Rinse onions under cold water; drain well. In medium mixing bowl, stir onions, tomatoes, cilantro, chiles, lime juice and salt. Let sit 10 to 15 minutes to blend flavors; gently stir in avocados. Serve as dip with corn chips.

SHRIMP-TOPPED DEVILED EGGS

Using jazzed-up Thousand Island dressing creates a quick shortcut to the flavors of a New Orleans-style remoulade sauce. This classic sauce pairs fabulously with shrimp and eggs.

6	eggs
¼	cup Thousand Island dressing
2	teaspoons stone-ground mustard
½	teaspoon dry mustard
¼	teaspoon salt
⅛	teaspoon hot pepper sauce
12	shelled, deveined cooked medium shrimp
12	sprigs parsley

6 servings.
Preparation time: 20 minutes.
Ready to serve: 45 minutes.

1 Fill medium saucepan half full of water; bring to a boil over medium-high heat. Ease eggs, in their shell, into water, using large spoon. Cook 14 minutes, regulating heat to maintain gentle boil once water returns to boiling. Remove immediately from heat; drain. Run eggs under cold running water until room temperature.

2 Shell eggs; slice in half lengthwise. Remove yolks; mash yolks in medium bowl with back of fork. In small bowl, whisk together dressing, mustards, salt and hot sauce; stir into egg yolks until smooth and well blended. Place 1 tablespoon of the egg yolk mixture evenly into cavity of each cooked egg-white half; top each with shrimp. Garnish with parsley.

*E*tching glass is a quick and easy way to give your old glassware new flare. These decorative wine glasses add a festive touch to your dinner party. Use any motif to fit your occasion. Etching a common design on mismatched glasses is a great way to tie them all together. Or use a design that complements a pattern on your dinnerware.

MATERIALS AND TOOLS

❑ GLASSWARE
❑ JUMBO DRAGONFLY CRAFT PUNCH
❑ CLEAR CONTACT PAPER
❑ GLASS ETCHING CREAM
❑ GLOVES
❑ SCISSORS

DIRECTIONS

1 Punch several dragonflies onto contact paper. Cut around the shape, leaving enough paper to apply the etching cream. Cut three dragonflies for each glass.

2 Peel off the paper backing and place the dragonflies to the front of the glass. Rub them firmly onto the glass, especially along the inside edge of the template.

3 Follow the directions for the etching cream. In a well-ventilated area, wearing rubber gloves, apply a layer of etching cream over the template. Leave on 5 minutes. Rinse off under running water and peel the contact paper off. Wash the glass with soap and water.

GRILLED ONION POTATO SALAD

You've never experienced a better-tasting potato salad than this! Your guests will flip!

1	medium-large onion
1	tablespoon olive oil
⅓	cup milk
1	teaspoon cider vinegar
½	cup mayonnaise
½	teaspoon salt
¼	teaspoon freshly ground pepper
2	lb. red boiling potatoes, about 5 or 6 medium
1	cup sliced celery

8 (1-cup) servings.
Preparation time: 40 minutes.
Ready to serve: 2 hours, 40 minutes.

1 Heat grill.

2 Slice onion into slightly larger than ¼ inch slices; brush both sides with olive oil. Place onion slices on charcoal grill 4 to 6 inches from medium coals or on gas grill over medium heat. Cook 4 to 5 minutes per side or until browned and tender. Let cool; chop into ¼-inch dice.

3 In large bowl, stir milk and vinegar together. Let sit 1 or 2 minutes to thicken. Whisk in mayonnaise, salt and pepper; stir in onions.

4 Cut potatoes into quarters. In large saucepan, bring potatoes to a boil in salted water over medium-high heat. Cook 20 to 25 minutes or until just tender; drain. When cool enough to handle, peel, if desired, and cut into ¾-inch dice; add to bowl with dressing. Add celery; stir gently to coat. Refrigerate, covered. Let chill several hours before serving.

MAPLE-MUSTARD COLESLAW

Maple and mustard work together for just the right zippy sweetness in this creamy coleslaw. For best results, use real maple syrup and not pancake syrup with maple flavoring.

⅔	cup mayonnaise
2	tablespoons Dijon mustard
2	tablespoons cider vinegar
½	cup maple syrup
1	(16-oz.) pkg. prepared coleslaw blend

6 servings.
Preparation time: 5 minutes.
Ready to serve: 25 minutes.

1 In large bowl, whisk together mayonnaise, mustard and cider vinegar. Whisk in maple syrup. Stir in coleslaw blend until mixture is evenly coated. Refrigerate, covered, 20 minutes before serving. Stir again just before serving to blend in released moisture from cabbage.

THREE BEAN SALAD WITH GAZPACHO VINAIGRETTE

Instead of the customary three bean salad with canned beans, this recipe uses the season's freshest produce combined with edamame beans. A nutrient powerhouse with a delightful taste and pleasant crunch, you can purchase these fresh soybeans raw in pods to be steamed or boiled, or you can get them already cooked and shelled.

GAZPACHO VINAIGRETTE

¼	cup tomato-based vegetable juice (V-8)
1½	teaspoons sherry wine vinegar
¼	teaspoon salt
⅛	teaspoon hot pepper sauce
2	tablespoons extra-virgin olive oil
1	medium tomato, diced

SALAD

½	lb. green beans, trimmed and cut in 1-inch pieces (about 1 cup)
½	lb. yellow wax beans, trimmed and cut in 1-inch pieces (about 1 cup)
1	cup cooked, shelled edamame beans (fresh soybeans)
6	lettuce leaves

6 servings.
Preparation time: 10 minutes.
Ready to serve: 20 minutes.

1 For Vinaigrette: In small bowl, stir vegetable juice, vinegar, salt and hot pepper sauce together until salt dissolves. Slowly stir in olive oil. Stir in diced tomato.

2 For Salad: Fill medium saucepan half full with water; bring to a boil over medium-high heat. Add green and yellow beans; cook 5 minutes or until crisp tender. Drain; run under cold water to stop cooking. Combine in medium bowl with edamame beans.

3 Just before serving, line 6 salad plates with lettuce leaves. Toss vinaigrette with beans; spoon over lettuce leaves.

SPINACH AND SMOKED TROUT SALAD WITH CHIVE VINAIGRETTE

Smoked fish adds a rich accent of flavor to the fresh, clean taste of spinach. Smoked whiting or hot-smoked salmon would work equally as well as trout here.

VINAIGRETTE

3	tablespoons lemon juice
2	teaspoons Dijon mustard
¼	teaspoon salt
¼	teaspoon freshly ground pepper
6	tablespoons chopped fresh chives
½	cup canola oil

SALAD

6	cups torn spinach leaves, stems removed
8	oz. sliced mushrooms
10	oz. whole smoked trout, skinned, boned, broken into pieces (about 1½ cups)

6 servings.
Preparation time: 15 minutes.
Ready to serve: 15 minutes.

1 For Vinaigrette: In small bowl, whisk together lemon juice, mustard, salt and pepper. Stir in 4 tablespoons of the chives. Slowly whisk in oil.

2 For Salad: In large bowl, toss spinach and mushrooms. Drizzle salad with vinaigrette; toss to coat. Divide evenly among 6 chilled salad plates. Scatter smoked trout evenly over each salad; sprinkle evenly with remaining 2 tablespoons fresh chives.

PASTA SALAD WITH GORGONZOLA DRESSING

Fresh produce, corkscrew pasta and a creamy gorgonzola dressing team up to make a delightful summer salad. Blanching the vegetables briefly in boiling water sets their color and enhances their taste. To make putting the dressing together a snap, choose a gorgonzola cheese that is firm enough to crumble easily.

1½	cups fusilli (corkscrew pasta)
1	cup (½-inch-diced) broccoli pieces
1	cup (½-inch-diced) carrot pieces
1	cup (½-inch-diced) yellow squash pieces
⅓	cup chopped red onion
¾	cup mayonnaise
¾	cup buttermilk
1	cup (4 oz.) crumbled domestic Gorgonzola cheese

6 servings.
Preparation time: 20 minutes.
Ready to serve: 3 hours, 20 minutes.

1 Cook fusilli in boiling water according to package directions. Drain; rinse under cold water. Drain again.

2 Meanwhile, bring large saucepan half full of water to a boil over medium-high heat. Add broccoli and carrots; cook 1 minute. Add yellow squash; cook an additional 1 minute. Drain; rinse under cold water. Drain well.

3 Rinse red onion under cold water; drain.

4 In large bowl, stir mayonnaise and buttermilk together; stir in Gorgonzola cheese. Add fusilli, lightly cooked vegetables and red onion; stir to combine. Refrigerate, covered, several hours to blend flavors, stirring occasionally. (Salad will appear a bit runny when first combined with dressing. The pasta will absorb the dressing as it chills.)

*H*ere is a charming way to add a creative touch to your drink napkins. Make a set of personalized cocktail napkins to use at your next holiday celebration. It is best to choose a stamp that has simple line work. Detailed stamps will not work as well. The dragonfly makes the pictured napkin a summery affair. Use a snowflake stamp for wintertime, or colored leaves for fall.

MATERIALS AND TOOLS

❑ COCKTAIL NAPKINS
❑ EMBROIDERY FLOSS
❑ STAMPING INK
❑ RUBBER STAMP
❑ SPRING HOOP
❑ NEEDLE
❑ SCISSORS
❑ SPONGE

DIRECTIONS

1 Ink the rubber stamp using a color that matches the embroidery floss. Stamp the napkin.

2 Insert the napkin into the spring hoop.

3 Use three strands of floss. Stitch along the line, using a backstitch. After the design has been completed, remove the ink with a wet sponge.

GRILLED PORK TENDERLOIN WITH ITALIAN RUB

Grilling over indirect heat means that the part of the grill used for cooking does not have a flame of hot coals directly below it. Either heat one side of a gas grill and cook on the other, or mound coals on either side of a charcoal grill and cook on the surface in between.

1	tablespoon chopped fresh rosemary
1	tablespoon chopped garlic
1	teaspoon dried oregano leaves
½	teaspoon dried thyme
½	teaspoon dried rubbed sage
¼	teaspoon salt
¼	teaspoon freshly ground pepper
2	(1- to 1¼-lb.) pork tenderloins

6 servings.
Preparation time: 10 minutes.
Ready to serve: 35 minutes.

1 Heat grill for indirect cooking.

2 Finely chop together rosemary, garlic, oregano, thyme, sage, salt and pepper. Rub into surface of pork tenderloins.

3 Place tenderloins on charcoal or gas grill over medium indirect heat; grill 25 to 35 minutes or until internal temperature reaches 155°F. Let rest 5 minutes; slice and serve.

CHERRY-BALSAMIC GLAZED CHICKEN BREASTS

Choose a quality brand of cherry preserves. Try the glaze on pork as well.

1	tablespoon olive oil
3	tablespoons minced shallots
¾	cup cherry preserves
¼	cup balsamic vinegar
¼	teaspoon Italian seasoning
⅛	teaspoon freshly ground pepper
6	boneless skinless chicken breasts
½	teaspoon salt

6 servings.
Preparation time: 10 minutes.
Ready to serve: 30 minutes.

1 Heat grill. In medium saucepan, heat olive oil over medium heat until hot. Add shallots; sauté until softened, about 3 to 4 minutes. Add cherry preserves, balsamic vinegar, Italian seasoning and pepper. Reduce heat to medium-low; cook until reduced by one-fourth, about 6 to 8 minutes. Reserve 6 tablespoons of glaze in small bowl.

2 Season chicken breasts with salt. Place chicken on charcoal grill 4 to 6 inches from medium coals or on gas grill over medium heat. Cook, covered, 4 minutes per side, turning once. Brush one side with remaining glaze; turn and brush other side. Spoon 1 tablespoon of reserved glaze over each breast. Cook an additional 2 to 3 minutes per side or until chicken is no longer pink in center.

GRILLED HERBED WALLEYE IN FOIL PACKETS

Feel free to substitute any mild, fresh white fish for the walleye in this recipe. Fish takes particularly well to cooking in packets, where plenty of natural moisture steams the fillets to succulent perfection.

6	(7- to 10-oz.) walleye fillets
3	tablespoons chopped chives
3	tablespoons chopped Italian parsley
1½	teaspoons fennel seeds, chopped
½	teaspoon salt
¼	teaspoon freshly ground pepper
2	tablespoons extra-virgin olive oil
6	lemon wedges

6 servings.
Preparation time: 15 minutes.
Ready to serve: 25 minutes.

1 Heat grill.

2 Spray 6 (18x12-inch) sheets of heavy-duty aluminum foil with nonstick cooking spray. Place one fillet in center of each sheet, tucking thinner portions of fillet under to form more even thickness.

3 In small bowl, blend chives and parsley; sprinkle evenly over fish. Sprinkle fish with chopped fennel seeds, salt and pepper. Drizzle each fillet with 1 teaspoon of olive oil. Wrap each fillet into packet, double-folding each seam and allowing room for steam expansion.

4 Place foil packets on charcoal grill 4 to 6 inches from medium coals or on gas grill over medium heat. Grill, covered, 9 to 11 minutes or until fish flakes easily with a fork and is no longer transparent in center. (Remove packets and carefully open one to test; if fish is not done, carefully reseal and return packets to grill.) Carefully open packets and remove fish to dinner plates, pouring cooking juices from packets over fish. Drizzle each portion evenly with fresh lemon.

PIGS IN A BLANKET WITH HOMEMADE BISCUIT DOUGH

This tasty combination of biscuit dough and sausages isn't just for children. Wrap up beer-braised brats for the adults and regular hot dogs for the kids. Make them earlier and bake just before serving for a fuss-free main course. Serve with mustard and ketchup for dipping and pickle spears for added crunch.

4	links smoked bratwurst
1	(12-oz.) bottle beer
1	small onion, quartered
2	cups all-purpose flour
2	teaspoons baking powder
¾	teaspoon salt
¼	cup shortening
⅔	cup plus 1 to 2 tablespoons milk
4	hot dogs

8 servings.
Preparation time: 20 minutes.
Ready to serve: 1 hour.

1 Heat oven to 425°F. Spray 17x13-inch baking sheet with nonstick cooking spray.

2 In large saucepan, heat bratwurst with beer and onion over medium heat until boiling. Reduce heat to low; simmer 15 minutes. Remove bratwurst and let cool.

3 Meanwhile, in medium bowl, stir together flour, baking powder and salt. Cut in shortening, using a pastry blender or two forks, until mixture resembles coarse sand. Add ⅔ cup milk, stirring until mixture comes together, adding 1 or 2 extra tablespoons if necessary to bring mixture into a ball.

4 Turn dough out onto lightly floured surface; knead 8 to 10 times. Roll dough to ¼ inch thickness. Cut dough into 4 (5x4-inch) rectangles and 4 (3x4-inch) rectangles. Roll cooled bratwursts in 5x4-inch rectangles, pinching seams closed; roll hot dogs in 3x4-inch rectangles, pinching seams closed. Arrange on prepared baking sheet. Bake 14 to 16 minutes or until lightly browned and the dough is cooked through.

Cajun Barbecued Ribs

These ribs start with a Cajun rub and finish with a saucy glaze. Slow cooking makes them fall-off-the-bone tender. Perfect for a summer get-together!

3	(1½- to 2-lb.) racks pork loin back ribs
5½	teaspoons Cajun seasoning
1	tablespoon celery salt
1	tablespoon garlic powder
1	tablespoon chili powder
1½	cups barbecue sauce

6 servings.
Preparation time: 15 minutes.
Ready to serve: 3 hours, 10 minutes.

1 Heat oven to 300°F. Line 2 jelly-roll pans with aluminum foil; spray with nonstick cooking spray.

2 Cut rib racks in half; pat dry and place on prepared pans. In small bowl, combine Cajun seasoning, celery salt, garlic powder and chili powder; sprinkle over both sides of ribs. Bake, meaty-side up, 2 hours. Brush both sides of ribs generously with barbecue sauce; bake an additional 20 minutes. Baste with barbecue sauce again; turn and bake an additional 20 minutes.

3 Meanwhile, heat grill. Place ribs on charcoal grill 4 to 6 inches from medium coals or on a gas grill over medium coals; baste with sauce and cook 7 minutes per side to char slightly.

Floral Vase
Place Card Holders

Create fragrant place card holders using miniature flower vases. This is a great way to use some of the flowers in your garden to dress up the dinner table. Use seasonal summer flowers to complement your party. In autumn, try using an assortment of chrysanthemums.

MATERIALS AND TOOLS

- ❏ FLOWERS
- ❏ MINIATURE VASES
- ❏ DECORATIVE PEBBLES (OPTIONAL)
- ❏ PLAIN WHITE VELLUM PAPER
- ❏ DECORATIVE VELLUM PAPER
- ❏ CORD OR RIBBON
- ❏ EXTRA-FINE METALLIC MARKER
- ❏ ⅛-INCH HOLE PUNCH
- ❏ SCISSORS
- ❏ PENCIL

DIRECTIONS

1 Draw the shape of a leaf on plain white vellum. Use scissors to cut the shape inside the drawn line.

2 Draw and cut a slightly larger leaf on decorative vellum paper. Use the smaller leaf as a guide for creating a larger leaf. Making different-size leaves will add visual interest.

3 Write a quest's name on the smaller leaf. Punch a hole through the two leaves. Tie the leaves to the vase with decorative cord or ribbon. Filling the vase with pebbles is optional. Place an arrangement of flowers in each vase.

NEW POTATO GRATIN

New potatoes are summer's freshly harvested, small red boiling potatoes with a delicate flavor. Large potatoes will work as well; just cut them into 1 to 1½-inch pieces before cooking. Leave the skins on as an added textural and nutritional bonus.

1	cup reduced-sodium chicken broth
1	large garlic clove, crushed
1	teaspoon olive oil
2	lb. small, red new potatoes, halved or quartered, depending on size
¼	teaspoon freshly ground pepper
1¼	(5 oz.) Gruyère or Emmentaler cheese, grated

6 servings.
Preparation time: 10 minutes.
Ready to serve: 60 minutes.

1 Heat oven to 400°F.

2 In small saucepan, bring chicken broth and garlic to a simmer over low heat. Grease 9-inch round or 11x7-inch glass or pottery baking dish with olive oil.

3 Add potatoes to prepared dish; sprinkle with pepper. Remove garlic clove from broth; pour broth over potatoes. Cover with aluminum foil; bake 20 minutes. Remove foil; sprinkle with cheese. Bake an additional 30 minutes or until cheese is melted and golden brown and potatoes are tender.

BETTER-THAN-HOMEMADE BAKED BEANS

These beans taste better than if you made them from scratch! Begin with your favorite brand of canned baked beans and perk up the flavor with extra goodness.

1	(28-oz.) can baked beans
1	(16-oz.) can baked beans
3	slices bacon, cooked, crumbled
3	tablespoons packed brown sugar
2	tablespoons molasses
2	tablespoons Bourbon (optional)
1	small onion, peeled

1 Place baked beans, bacon, sugar, molasses and Bourbon in bottom of 3½- to 4-quart slow cooker; stir to combine. Place onion in center of beans. Cook, covered, on low heat 5 to 6 hours or on high heat 2½ to 3 hours. Remove onion.

8 to 10 servings.
Preparation time: 5 minutes.
Ready to serve: 2 hours, 35 minutes.

APPLE-PECAN CORN MUFFINS

You can't get better muffins than these when they're made totally from scratch. But if you're in a rush, add the apples and pecans to a prepared corn muffin mix.

1½	cups all-purpose flour
½	cup corn meal
2	tablespoons sugar
2	teaspoons baking powder
½	teaspoon baking soda
½	teaspoon salt
½	teaspoon dried rubbed sage
1	cup chopped Granny Smith apples
½	cup chopped pecans
1	cup buttermilk
3	tablespoons butter, melted, cooled
1	egg

1 Heat oven to 400°F. Spray 12 muffin cups with nonstick cooking spray.

2 In medium mixing bowl, sift flour, cornmeal, sugar, baking powder, baking soda, salt and sage. Stir in apples and pecans. In another medium mixing bowl, mix together buttermilk, butter and egg; pour into flour mixture. Stir until just combined; do not overmix.

3 Spoon batter into prepared cups. Bake 20 minutes or until golden brown and toothpick inserted in center of muffin comes out clean.

12 muffins.
Preparation time: 15 minutes.
Ready to serve: 35 minutes.

ZUCCHINI-CORN SAUTE

Here's the recipe to turn to when "the season" hits. Paired with abundant zucchini and a simple garlic and butter topping, the fresh sweet flavor of each golden kernel of corn shines through.

1	tablespoon olive oil
½	medium red onion, cut into ½-inch dice
1	teaspoon balsamic vinegar
2	small zucchini (about quarter sized in diameter), cut into ½-inch dice
1½	cups fresh corn kernels (2 to 3 ears)
1	tablespoon minced garlic
2	tablespoons butter
¼	teaspoon salt
⅛	teaspoon freshly ground pepper

6 (½-cup) servings.
Preparation time: 15 minutes.
Ready to serve: 25 minutes.

1 In large skillet, heat oil over medium-high heat until hot. Add red onion; sauté 3 to 4 minutes or until softened. Stir in balsamic vinegar. Add zucchini; sauté 2 minutes. Add corn; sauté an additional 2 to 3 minutes or until corn is crisp tender. Stir in garlic; cook 30 seconds to 1 minute or until aromatic. Remove from heat; stir in butter, salt and pepper.

ROSEMARY FOCACCIA

Try topping this bread with caramelized onions, chopped walnuts or any variety of herbs for a change of pace. The crunchy exterior and tender interior make this quick bread a real winner.

½	cup water
¼	cup milk
3	tablespoons potato flakes or buds
1	tablespoon plus 2 teaspoons extra-virgin olive oil
2	teaspoons finely minced rosemary
2	cups unbleached flour
1	(¼-oz.) pkg. quick-rise yeast
1	teaspoon sugar
½	teaspoon plus ⅛ teaspoon salt

6 servings.
Preparation time: 20 minutes.
Ready to serve: 2 hours.

1 In small saucepan, heat water and milk to 120°F to 130°F over low heat; remove to small bowl. Add potato flakes; stir to blend. Stir in 1 tablespoon olive oil and 1 teaspoon rosemary; let rest 5 minutes.

2 In medium bowl, combine 1¾ cups flour, yeast, sugar and ½ teaspoon salt; stir in milk mixture to make soft dough. Sprinkle remaining ¼ cup flour on counter; turn dough out onto lightly floured surface. Knead briefly until dough just starts to become elastic, about 3 to 4 minutes, working flour on surface as necessary to keep dough from sticking. Let rest 10 minutes.

3 Grease 9-inch glass pie pan with 1 teaspoon of olive oil; turn dough into prepared pan. Rub surface of dough with remaining 1 teaspoon olive oil and using fingertips, press dough flat in pan. Let rise until double in bulk, about 30 to 45 minutes.

4 Meanwhile, heat oven to 400°F. Chop remaining 1 teaspoon rosemary with remaining ⅛ teaspoon of salt to blend. When dough has risen, press fingertips gently into surface in several places to create dimples. Sprinkle surface with rosemary-salt mixture. Bake 20 to 25 minutes or until well browned. With spatula, lift focaccia from pan; let cool on wire rack before slicing.

OCEANIC CANDLE HOLDER

*I*nspired by summers at the beach, these tranquil centerpieces will add a serene touch to your party. They will work great for indoor or outdoor events. Place two or three across a table for a dramatic effect. Try floating flowers instead of using candles.

MATERIALS AND TOOLS

- ❏ GLASS HURRICANE CONTAINER
- ❏ SAND
- ❏ SEASHELLS
- ❏ FLOATING CANDLE

DIRECTIONS

1 Fill the container about a quarter full of sand. Place various seashells on top, slightly pushing them into the sand.

2 Fill the container with water. Pour the water over your hand, to avoid disturbing the sand. Leave enough room to accommodate a lit candle.

3 Allow the sand to settle for a few hours or until the water is clear. Place a floating candle in the container, and light.

RED, WHITE AND BLUEBERRY SHORTCAKES

These shortcakes are particularly tender and offer an added bonus: chunks of white chocolate tucked inside the scone-like dough.

SHORTCAKES

1⅔	cups all-purpose flour
2¼	teaspoons baking powder
¼	teaspoon salt
6	tablespoons cold, unsalted butter, cut in ½-inch dice
3	oz. white chocolate, cut in chunks
¼	cup sugar
½	cup heavy whipping cream
1	egg

FILLING

1½	cups heavy whipping cream
1	oz. white chocolate, chopped
1	pint strawberries, halved or 1 pint raspberries
1	pint blueberries

6 servings.
Preparation time: 25 minutes.
Ready to serve: 1 hour, 10 minutes.

1 Heat oven to 375°F. Lightly spray baking sheet with nonstick cooking spray.

2 For Shortcakes: In medium bowl, blend together flour, baking powder and salt. Cut in butter, using pastry blender or two forks, until mixture resembles coarse sand. Stir in 3 oz. white chocolate chunks and sugar. In small bowl, whisk together ½ cup cream and egg. Stir cream mixture into flour mixture until just combined.

3 Turn mixture onto lightly floured surface; pat to 1 inch thickness. Cut with a 2½-inch-round cutter into 6 circles, working scraps together if necessary to form all the circles. Place on prepared baking sheet; bake 20 to 25 minutes or until lightly browned. Let cool on wire rack. Split in two while still slightly warm and the white chocolate has not completely hardened.

4 For Filling: In medium, microwave-proof bowl, combine ¼ cup whipping cream and 1 oz. chopped white chocolate. Melt chocolate on Medium power, about 1 minute; stir to combine. Let cool 30 minutes, stirring occasionally.

5 In medium bowl, whip remaining 1¼ cups whipping cream with mixer on high speed until slightly firmer than soft peaks form. Slowly beat in cooled, melted white chocolate to form a soft cream filling. Refrigerate, covered, until ready to serve; stir gently before serving.

6 When ready to serve, place bottom halves of shortcakes on 6 dessert plates. Spoon white chocolate whipped cream over bottoms; top with fruit. Cover with top halves of shortcakes; serve immediately.

S'MORE ICE CREAM SANDWICHES

If you don't have a campfire, brown the tiny marshmallows quickly under the broiler to give these s'more sandwiches the proper taste.

3	cups mini marshmallows
8	full graham cracker sheets
1	half-gallon chocolate ice cream, in rectangular carton

8 servings.
Preparation time: 25 minutes.
Ready to serve: 25 minutes.

1 Heat broiler.

2 Line 15x10-inch baking sheet with aluminum foil; spray with nonstick cooking spray. Sprinkle half of mini marshmallows over baking sheet, keeping as separate as possible. Broil 30 seconds to 1 minute or until a deep brown. Gently lift foil and let cool on foil; repeat process with remaining marshmallows using cool baking sheet.

3 Split graham cracker sheets in half to form 16 squares.

4 Cut rectangular carton of ice cream in half, using serrated knife. Wrap one half in plastic wrap and freeze for later use. Remove carton wrapper from ice cream; cut ice cream in 4 slices. Cut each slice in half to form a total of 8 squares. Place each ice cream square on top of a graham cracker square; top ice cream with a second graham cracker square to form a sandwich. Place on baking sheet in the freezer.

5 Working with one sandwich at a time, gently lift the toasted mini marshmallows, a few at a time, from the aluminum foil and press untoasted sides into edges of ice cream to cover all edges. Return to freezer and repeat with remaining sandwiches. Freeze, covered with plastic wrap, until ready to serve.

PEACH COBBLER

Since it contains just the right amount of leavening, self-rising flour makes this recipe a breeze. Just add butter and liquid for a wonderful cobbler topping. During the summer, when fruit is plentiful, feel free to combine the peaches with other fruits. You can substitute 2 cups of berries for an equal amount of peaches. Use nectarines instead of peaches for another variation.

6	tablespoons sugar
2	tablespoons cornstarch
½	cup packed brown sugar
6	cups sliced peaches or 1½ (16-oz.) bags frozen peaches, thawed
1	¾ cup self-rising flour
4	tablespoons (¼ cup) chilled unsalted butter, cut in cubes
½	cup heavy whipping cream
½	cup buttermilk
½	teaspoon almond extract

6 to 8 servings.
Preparation time: 15 minutes.
Ready to serve: 1 hour, 45 minutes.

1 Heat oven to 375°F.

2 In large bowl, stir 4 tablespoons of sugar and cornstarch together until well blended; stir in brown sugar. Add peaches; toss to coat. Let sit 10 minutes to release juices; spoon peach-sugar mixture into 9-inch round glass or ceramic baking dish or deep-dish pie pan. Place on aluminum foil-lined baking sheet. Bake 25 minutes.

3 Meanwhile, in medium bowl, combine remaining 2 tablespoons sugar and self-rising flour. Cut in butter, using pastry blender or two forks, until mixture resembles coarse sand. Stir cream, buttermilk and almond extract together in small bowl; stir into flour mixture just until combined. Drop by spoonfuls on top of hot peaches. Bake an additional 35 minutes or until top is browned and peach juices are thickened and bubbling. Let cool to lukewarm or serve at room temperature.

MELON SORBET

Look for a cantaloupe that is as ripe as possible. It should feel heavy for its size, smell like melon without being overwhelming, and yield slightly at its stem end when pressed.

1	cup sugar
1	cup water
1¼	cups pureed ripe cantaloupe
¼	cup orange juice
1	tablespoon lime juice

6 servings (about ½ cup per serving).
Preparation time: 10 minutes.
Ready to serve: 6 hours, 40 minutes.

1 In medium saucepan, combine sugar and water; bring to a boil over medium-high heat, stirring frequently. Reduce heat to low and simmer about 1 to 2 minutes or until all sugar is dissolved. Remove from heat; transfer to medium metal bowl and refrigerate 3 hours.

2 When chilled, add cantaloupe, orange juice and lime juice; stir to blend. Pour into ice cream maker and process according to manufacturer's directions, about 25 to 30 minutes or until softly set.

3 Meanwhile, place medium metal bowl in freezer; when sorbet is set, transfer to chilled bowl and return to freezer, covered, 3 hours or until firm.

SEMIFREDDO TIRAMISU TORTE

Semifreddo means half cold or half frozen in Italian. That perfectly describes the consistency of this dessert. You can make it a day ahead and freeze; just remove the torte from the freezer about 45 minutes before serving. This pretty torte is great on its own or served with fresh strawberries for a garnish.

1	(3-oz.) pkg. vanilla cook-and-serve pudding mix
2	cups milk
2	tablespoons amber rum
1	(8-oz.) container mascarpone cheese, at room temperature
¾	cup water
6	tablespoons sugar
1½	teaspoons instant coffee granules
¼	cup coffee-flavored liqueur
1	cup heavy whipping cream
2	(3-oz.) pkg. ladyfingers*
1½	teaspoons unsweetened cocoa

10 to 12 servings.
Preparation time: 1hour, 55 minutes.
Ready to serve: 4 hours, 55 minutes.

1 In medium saucepan, whisk pudding mix into milk. Heat over medium heat, stirring constantly, until mixture comes to a full boil. Remove from heat; stir in rum. Let rest 5 minutes, stirring 2 times.

2 In medium bowl, gently whisk ¼ cup of pudding with the mascarpone until smooth; whisk in remaining pudding. Cover with plastic wrap applied directly to surface of mascarpone mixture. Refrigerate until chilled, about 1½ hours.

3 Meanwhile, in medium saucepan, combine water and 4 tablespoons of sugar; bring to a boil over medium heat until sugar dissolves. Remove from heat; stir in coffee crystals until dissolved. Stir in liqueur; set aside to cool.

4 When mascarpone mixture has chilled, whip cream in medium bowl with mixer on medium speed until soft peaks form. Whip in remaining 2 tablespoons sugar until cream is almost stiff. Fold one third of whipped cream into mascarpone mixture with whisk until partially blended; repeat with next third. Add final third and fold, using large plastic spatula, until no streaks of whipped cream remain.

5 Trim ½ inch from bottom of ladyfingers from 1 package. Line 9-inch springform pan with trimmed ladyfingers standing upright around sides, trimmed-side down and flat sides inward. Line bottom with any remaining ladyfingers from first package, and part of the ladyfingers from the second package, filling in gaps with some of the trimmed ends. Brush ladyfingers, lining sides and bottom several times with coffee liquid to thoroughly coat but not soak through. Spoon half of mascarpone-whipped cream mixture into pan. Top with remaining ladyfingers and trimmed pieces.

6 Brush ladyfingers with coffee mixture to thoroughly coat. Place 1 teaspoon of cocoa in fine strainer; sprinkle over ladyfingers. Spoon remaining mascarpone-whipped cream mixture over all; spread to smooth. Freeze, covered, 4 hours to firm. Remove sides. Place remaining ½ teaspoon cocoa in strainer; sprinkle over top just before serving. Cut in wedges to serve. Store in refrigerator.

TIP* You can find ladyfingers in your local supermarket's bakery or in the cookie aisle.

INDIVIDUAL FRESH FRUIT TARTS

Vary this recipe by using your favorite jam instead of marmalade. Any small and fresh fruit works well here; for instance, try grapes and raspberries instead of strawberries and blueberries.

½	(17.3-oz.) pkg. frozen puff pastry, thawed
1½	teaspoon sugar
10	teaspoons orange marmalade
10	fresh strawberries, halved
20	fresh blueberries

10 tarts.
Preparation time: 15 minutes.
Ready to serve: 25 minutes.

1 Heat oven to 350°F. Line baking sheet with parchment paper; set aside.

2 Roll pastry on lightly-floured surface into 12x10-inch rectangle. Cut 10 circles from pastry, using 2½-inch round cutter; arrange circles on baking sheet.

3 Inside each circle, cut another circle using a 2-inch round cutter. Run finger dipped in water around edge of inner cut circle. Carefully lift edge of half of outer-ring pastry; invert to line up with outer edge of inner circle on the other side. Lift other half of outer ring; invert to line up with other edge to form case. (The overlapping portions form a decorative curlicue on each side). Gently press together to seal.

4 Repeat with remaining pastry. Prick inner area with tines of fork every ¼ inch. Sprinkle with sugar; bake 20 to 25 minutes or until crisp and brown. Let cool on wire rack.

5 Before serving, fill each tart with ½ teaspoon marmalade. Top with half of one strawberry and 2 blueberries.

Melon Skewers

Instead of serving a bowl of mixed fruit, try using these delightful skewers for a refreshing change. Use shape cutters on a variety of melons for a decorative presentation. Children will enjoy helping you with this step. Try packing these skewers in a container to bring to picnics.

MATERIALS AND TOOLS

❏ SKEWERS
❏ PAPER CLAY (AIR-DRY)
❏ ACRYLIC PAINT
❏ PAINTBRUSH

DIRECTIONS

1 Roll out a long coil of clay. Use a little water if the clay is drying out too quickly.

2 Wind a coil around the bottom of the skewer about 3 inches long. Allow it to dry for 24 hours. Use a cup full of sand or sugar to prop the skewers upright to dry.

3 Apply two coats of paint. Add a little water to thin the acrylic paint for a smoother finish.

fall HOLIDAYS

Harvest

Halloween

Thanksgiving

Birthday

Anniversary

Game Day

Election Day

Autumnal Equinox

CHERRY TOMATO TOASTS

At the end of tomato season, there are often hundreds of ripe, delicious cherry tomatoes just begging to be eaten. This is one simple way to use them. It's also a great way to coax children into eating something before trick-or-treating.

1	pint cherry tomatoes
⅛	teaspoon kosher (coarse) salt
⅛	teaspoon freshly ground pepper
8	slices hearth-style bread, toasted
4	garlic cloves, unpeeled, cut in half crosswise
¼	cup (1 oz.) freshly grated Parmigiano-Reggiano cheese
4	tablespoons extra-virgin olive oil
2	tablespoons snipped fresh chives or very thinly sliced fresh basil

Serves 4.

Preparation time: 10 minutes.

Ready to serve: 20 minutes.

1 Cut tomatoes in half and place in small bowl; season with salt and pepper.

2 Set bread on work surface; rub 1 piece of garlic over top side of each piece, pressing firmly to push garlic juice into bread.

3 Arrange two slices of bread on individual plates. Spoon cherry tomatoes evenly over each slice. Top with grated cheese; drizzle with olive oil. Sprinkle with chives or basil. Serve immediately.

SALT AND PEPPER BREADSTICKS WITH HERB BUTTER

Kids love making these breadsticks. For fun, turn them into other shapes!

BREADSTICKS

1	recipe prepared Pizza Dough (page 99)
½	cup all-purpose flour
1	egg white mixed with 1 tablespoon water
2	tablespoons medium-coarse sea salt, such as sel gris or Hawaiian alaea salt
1	tablespoon crushed black peppercorns
2	teaspoons crushed white peppercorns
¼	cup corn meal

HERB BUTTER

6	oz. unsalted butter, at room temperature
½	teaspoon kosher (coarse) salt
1	garlic clove, minced
1	tablespoon minced fresh Italian parsley
1	teaspoon each: minced fresh oregano, minced fresh thyme, snipped chives
½	teaspoon minced rosemary
⅛	teaspoon freshly ground pepper

16 breadsticks.
⅓ cup Herb Butter.
Preparation time: 35 minutes.
Ready to serve: 3 hours, 30 minutes.

1 After dough's first rise, let rest 10 minutes. Heat oven to 375°F.

2 Cut dough in half, then cut each piece in half again. Continue until you have 16 equal pieces.

3 Sprinkle work surface lightly with flour; rub a little of the flour on palms of hands. Roll one piece of dough between palms until it forms rope about 8 to 10 inches long; set rope on floured surface. Continue working dough with hands until you have formed all the ropes.

4 Brush each breadstick evenly with egg white mixture; sprinkle with salt and crushed peppercorns. Turn over; repeat.

5 Sprinkle insulated baking sheet with cornmeal; arrange breadsticks about ½ inch apart. Bake until lightly browned, about 12 minutes. Cool breadsticks on a wire rack; serve warm or at room temperature, with herb butter.

6 For Herb Butter: In small bowl, combine butter and salt. Add garlic, parsley, oregano, thyme, chives, rosemary and pepper; mix until smooth. Press butter mixture into a small ramekin; cover and refrigerate 30 minutes. Remove from refrigerator 30 minutes before serving. Herb butter will keep in refrigerator up to 3 or 4 days.

GRILLED PIZZA WITH TOMATOES AND FONTINA

When you grill pizza, use a clean grill rack so that the dough neither sticks nor burns.

PIZZA DOUGH

2	teaspoons active dry yeast
⅔	cup warm water
2½	cups all-purpose flour
1	teaspoon salt
4	teaspoons extra-virgin olive oil

TOPPINGS

4	tablespoons extra-virgin olive oil
3 to 4	garlic cloves, minced
⅛	teaspoon kosher (coarse) salt
⅛	teaspoon freshly ground pepper
2	cups (8 oz.) Italian fontina cheese
6	ripe plum tomatoes, cut into thin rounds (¼ inch thick)
3	tablespoons minced fresh herbs (oregano, Italian parsley, thyme, chives and basil)

Serves 6.

Preparation time: 25 minutes.
Ready to serve: 3 hours, 30 minutes.

1 To prepare Pizza Dough: In large mixing bowl, combine yeast and water; set aside 10 minutes. Stir in ½ cup flour, salt and olive oil. Add remaining flour, ½ cup at a time, until you have ½ cup remaining. Stir in half of remaining flour, reserving ¼ cup. Turn dough onto floured surface. Knead dough until smooth and velvety, about 7 minutes, working in as much of the remaining flour as dough will take.

2 Brush large, clean bowl lightly with olive oil. Set dough in bowl; cover with damp towel. Let dough rise 3 hours or until it has doubled in size. Gently turn dough onto lightly floured work surface; let rest 5 minutes.

3 Using heel of your hand, press dough into flat circle. Pick dough up holding it perpendicular to your work surface and move your hands around its outer edges, shaking gently as you do. If it doesn't stretch easily, put one hand on either side of the round and pull gently and flatten until dough is 12-inch round, about ⅜ inch thick.

4 Heat grill.

5 Cut dough in half. With your hands, slowly stretch both pieces into rounds. Place stretched dough on gas grill over medium heat or on charcoal grill 4 to 6 inches from medium coals until lightly toasted, about 1 to 2 minutes. Transfer to work surface, grilled-side up.

6 Drizzle each pizza with about 2 tablespoons of olive oil. Sprinkle garlic over oil. Season with salt and pepper. Sprinkle cheese on top, followed by tomatoes and herbs. Place pizza on grill; cook until cheese is melted and crusts are crisp, about 5 minutes. Cut into wedges and serve immediately.

MOZZARELLA FRESCA AND OLIVES WITH TOASTED BAGUETTES

Freshly made mozzarella is tender and delicate; it can also be a bit bland, so add a little salt directly to the cheese for more flavor.

1	lb. mozzarella fresca cheese, cut into ¼-inch-thick slices
1	cup olives (niçoise, picholine, lucques or kalamatas)
3	tablespoons extra-virgin olive oil
⅛	teaspoon freshly ground pepper
½	sourdough baguette, thinly sliced, toasted

1 Arrange mozzarella fresca cheese on serving platter. Sprinkle olives around cheese; drizzle with olive oil. Season with pepper. Arrange toasted baguettes around outer edge of platter. Serve within 30 minutes.

Serves 4.
Preparation time: 10 minutes.
Ready to serve: 10 minutes.

Dried Lunaria Candle Wreaths

The shimmering quality of this dried plant is complemented by warm candlelight. The ornamental part of the lunaria plant is found inside the seed pods, the fruit of the flowering plant. After it has dried, the pods are opened to reveal the silvery coin. Try using dried lavender to create a fragrant wreath.

MATERIALS AND TOOLS

❏ DRIED LUNARIA
❏ 1 FOOT 16-GAUGE WIRE
❏ EXTRA-FINE WIRE
❏ WIRE CUTTERS
❏ NEEDLENOSE PLIERS

DIRECTIONS

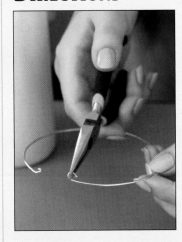

1 Make a circular frame to fit around the base of the candle. Use the needlenose pliers to bend a hook at each end of the wire to crimp together.

2 Group a few pieces of cut lunaria together and bind them around the circle with extra fine wire. Begin by wrapping the wire around the frame several times to anchor it in place.

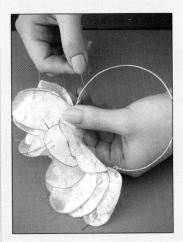

3 Continue around the frame, overlapping each bunch on top of the preceding one.

MARINATED MUSHROOMS WITH LEMON AND GARLIC

Serve these flavorful mushrooms with hot sourdough bread, which is perfect for sopping up any marinade that drips on the plate.

1	tablespoon kosher (coarse) salt
1	lb. small crimini mushrooms, washed, dried
1	½ cups extra-virgin olive oil
½	cup fresh lemon juice
8	garlic cloves, crushed
1	tablespoon minced Italian parsley
2	teaspoons fresh thyme
2	teaspoons mustard seeds
2	teaspoons whole black peppercorns

Serves 4.
Preparation time: 15 minutes.
Ready to serve: 1 hour, 25 minutes.

1 Fill medium saucepan with 2 quarts water. Add salt and mushrooms; bring to a boil over medium-high heat. Remove saucepan from heat. Let rest 5 minutes; drain thoroughly. Transfer mushrooms to medium ceramic bowl or crock.

2 In medium bowl, combine olive oil, lemon juice, garlic, parsley, thyme, mustard seeds and peppercorns; mix well. Pour mixture over mushrooms. Let rest at room temperature, covered, 1 hour. Refrigerate until 15 minutes before serving. Mushrooms will keep in refrigerator up to 4 or 5 days.

END-OF-SEASON TOMATO SALAD

There are two points to this salad: One: Use fall's tomatoes before the first freeze. Two: Discover new heirloom tomatoes. If you do not grow tomatoes yourself, the best place to find good ones is at your farmers' market.

10	medium tomatoes, preferably a mix of heirloom varieties, cut into 1-inch-wide wedges
6	small heirloom tomatoes, quartered
1	sweet onion, quartered, cut into paper-thin slices
4	garlic cloves, minced
⅛	teaspoon kosher (coarse) salt
3	tablespoons red wine vinegar
¼	cup extra-virgin olive oil
2	tablespoons capers
⅛	teaspoon freshly ground pepper
¼	cup basil leaves cut into ⅛-inch-thick strips

1 In large bowl, combine tomatoes, onions and garlic; toss. Season with salt; drizzle with vinegar. Cover and set aside 30 minutes.

2 Shortly before serving, drizzle olive oil over salad. Add capers and pepper; toss. Sprinkle basil over top; serve immediately.

Serves 4.
Preparation time: 15 minutes.
Ready to serve: 45 minutes.

FALL'S CHOPPED SALAD

Slicing or chopping the ingredients in a salad creates a very different effect than using whole or hand-torn leaves.

1	head romaine lettuce, cut into thin ½-inch strips
¼	head green cabbage, shredded
¼	head red cabbage, shredded
1	bunch watercress, stems trimmed, chopped
3	ribs celery, trimmed, cut into ¼-inch diagonal slices
2	tablespoons fresh mint, chopped
½	cup Italian parsley, chopped
⅛	teaspoon kosher (coarse) salt
3	tablespoons white wine vinegar
6	tablespoons extra-virgin olive oil
⅛	teaspoon freshly ground pepper
1	ripe pear, peeled, cored, cut into matchstick-size strips
½	cup pomegranate seeds

1 In large bowl, combine lettuce, cabbages, watercress, celery, mint and parsley; toss together. Sprinkle with salt; toss again.

2 In small bowl, mix together vinegar and olive oil. Season with pepper. Pour vinegar mixture over salad. Add pear; toss gently. Sprinkle pomegranate seeds over salad. Serve immediately.

Serves 4.
Preparation time: 15 minutes.
Ready to serve: 15 minutes.

BUTTER LETTUCE WITH BLUE CHEESE AND CROUTONS

Butter lettuce is the most tender and delicate of greens, hence its name, which evokes the texture of the innermost leaves. It grows well in the coolness of fall.

CROUTONS

4 to 5	slices hearth-style bread, cut into ¾-inch cubes
2 to 3	tablespoons olive oil
⅛	teaspoon kosher (coarse) salt
⅛	teaspoon freshly ground pepper

DRESSING

3 oz.	blue cheese
½	cup half-and-half
8	walnut halves, finely chopped
1	tablespoon fresh snipped chives
⅛	teaspoon freshly ground pepper

SALAD

4	large heads of butter lettuce
2	tablespoons fresh-squeezed lemon juice or 1 tablespoon white wine or Champagne vinegar

Serves 4.
Preparation time: 15 minutes.
Ready to serve: 35 minutes.

1 Heat oven to 300°F.

2 For Croutons: Place bread cubes in large bowl; drizzle with olive oil. Sprinkle with salt and pepper. Toss until olive oil is evenly distributed and absorbed. Pour cubes into 13x9-inch pan; bake until golden brown, about 20 minutes.

3 Meanwhile, prepare Dressing: In small bowl, mash cheese with fork. Add half-and-half, then mix. Add walnuts, chives and pepper; mix.

4 For Salad: Remove outer leaves of lettuce, leaving just tender hearts. Rinse in cool water. Stir lemon juice into dressing. Spoon dressing over lettuce. Scatter croutons over salad; serve immediately.

FALL'S GREENS WITH AVOCADO AND GRAPEFRUIT

The combination of avocado and grapefruit is utterly seductive!

1	grapefruit, peeled, pith removed
1	small shallot, minced
⅛	teaspoon salt
⅛	teaspoon freshly ground pepper
1	tablespoon Champagne or white wine vinegar
⅓	cup mild olive oil
5	cups fresh fall greens
1	firm-ripe avocado, cut into lengthwise slices

Serves 4.
Preparation time: 20 minutes.
Ready to serve: 30 minutes.

1 Hold peeled grapefruit over large bowl to catch juice. Slice close to each membrane to loosen and remove each segment. Squeeze membrane to remove any remaining juice. Reserve 3 tablespoons of the juice to make vinaigrette. Set segments aside.

2 In small bowl, season shallot with salt; stir in vinegar and grapefruit juice. Set aside 15 minutes. Add olive oil; season with pepper.

3 Place greens in large bowl; drizzle with half of the dressing; toss to coat.

4 Arrange avocado slices and grapefruit sections on individual salad plates. Mound greens in center of plate. Spoon some of the remaining dressing over the avocado and grapefruit; serve immediately.

BEADED WIRE
NAPKIN RINGS

Make your own beaded napkin rings easily. Visit your local bead store to find a great selection of natural gemstones to create a stylish set. The glass beads chosen for this napkin ring complement colors found in autumn. Match them to your linens or dishware.

MATERIALS AND TOOLS

- ❏ ASSORTED BEADS
- ❏ BRACELET MEMORY WIRE (3½ COILS)
- ❏ NEEDLENOSE PLIERS
- ❏ WIRE CUTTERS

DIRECTIONS

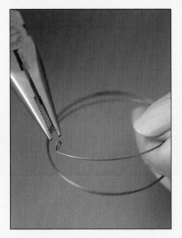

1 Make a little loop at one end of the wire using needlenose pliers. Bend the loop at a 90-degree angle so the loop will be right up against the bead.

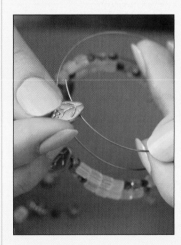

2 Selectively place the beads onto the wire.

3 Complete three rows of beads and cut the excess wire. Make another little loop at the end of the wire. Bend the wire at a 90-degree angle to finish.

FALL RICE SALAD WITH POMEGRANATES, AVOCADO AND WALNUTS

Texture is nearly as important as flavor in this colorful salad; the contrast between creamy avocado, crunchy toasted walnuts and sweet pomegranates is very appealing.

RICE

1¼	cups water
1	teaspoon kosher (coarse) salt
¾	cup jasmine or basmati rice
	Juice of 1 lemon
⅛	teaspoon salt
⅛	teaspoon freshly ground pepper

POMEGRANATE VINAIGRETTE

1	small shallot, minced
1	tablespoon Champagne vinegar
¼	cup fresh pomegranate juice (pressed from about ⅔ cup seeds)
	Peel of ½ lemon
	Dash of sugar
⅛	teaspoon kosher (coarse) salt
⅛	teaspoon freshly ground pepper
½	cup unrefined walnut oil or mildly flavored olive oil

SALAD

8	scallions, trimmed, thinly sliced
	Seeds from 2 pomegranates
	Peel of 1 lemon, grated
4	tablespoons minced fresh cilantro (or 2 tablespoons minced Italian parsley and 2 tablespoons snipped chives)
1	large firm-ripe avocado, cut in half lengthwise
½	cup walnut pieces, lightly toasted

Serves 4.
⅔ cup Vinaigrette.
Preparation time: 20 minutes.
Ready to serve: 50 minutes.

1 For Rice: Pour 1¼ cups water into heavy saucepan. Add salt and rice; bring water to a rolling boil over high heat. Reduce heat to low; cover pan and simmer 15 minutes. Remove pan from heat; steam rice, covered and undisturbed, 15 minutes. Transfer rice to wide, shallow bowl; fluff with fork. Cool to room temperature.

2 Pour lemon juice over rice; toss. Season with salt and pepper; toss again. Set aside.

3 For Vinaigrette: In medium bowl, combine shallots and vinegar. Add pomegranate juice, lemon peel, sugar, salt and pepper. Whisk in oil; add another pinch of sugar if necessary to boost pomegranate flavor.

4 For Salad: Add scallions, half of the pomegranate seeds, lemon peel and cilantro to the rice; toss together. Pour about two-thirds of the vinaigrette over the salad; toss again.

5 Cut avocado into medium dice. Add diced avocado and walnuts to salad; toss very gently. Season with salt and pepper, if necessary. Pour remaining dressing over salad and sprinkle with remaining pomegranate seeds.

BEEF SHANKS AND GARLIC BRAISED IN RED WINE

Like slow-cooked lamb or pork, slow-cooked beef develops rich, sweet flavors and luscious textures that are perfect when fall's chill is in the air.

2 to 3	tablespoons olive oil
12	garlic cloves
4 to 5	lb. beef shanks, cut into 1½ to 2-inch-thick pieces
⅛	teaspoon kosher (coarse) salt
⅛	teaspoon freshly ground pepper
3	leeks, white and pale green parts only, cut into ½-inch-thick rounds
3	cups red wine
3	cups veal or beef stock
2	to 3 thyme sprigs

Serves 4.
Preparation time: 30 minutes.
Ready to serve: 2 hours, 30 minutes.

1 Heat oven to 325°F.

2 In Dutch oven, heat oil over medium-high heat until hot. Add garlic; sauté 4 to 6 minutes or until softened. With slotted spoon, transfer garlic to small bowl; set aside.

3 Season shanks with salt and pepper. Add to Dutch oven; brown on both sides. Transfer shanks to plate. Add leeks; sauté until wilted, about 8 to 9 minutes. Return garlic to Dutch oven; place shanks on top. Pour in wine and stock; add thyme. Increase heat to high. When liquid comes to boil, remove from heat, cover and place in oven; bake 90 minutes.

4 Remove lid and cook an additional 30 minutes or until shanks are fork-tender. Remove from oven; cover and let rest 20 minutes.

5 Arrange shanks on platter; top with garlic. Serve remaining juices with shanks; serve immediately.

MIXED VEGETABLE AND SAUSAGE GRILL WITH PARSLEY VINAIGRETTE

In the fall, a frenzy of fresh vegetables must be enjoyed immediately or lost. This recipe celebrates that harvest. It's an excellent way to involve kids, as even a toddler can help thread tomatoes onto skewers. Chop leftover grilled vegetables and toss with some of the vinaigrette for an excellent salad, or heat and serve over pasta.

MIXED VEGETABLES

2	lb. fresh Italian sausage links
12	small new potatoes
3	tablespoons kosher (coarse) salt
3	medium onions, peeled, cut in half lengthwise
¼	cup olive oil
3	large eggplants, cut into ⅜-inch-thick lengthwise slices
3 to 4	(6-inch-long) zucchini, cut in half lengthwise
⅛	teaspoon freshly ground pepper
1	lb. crimini mushrooms
2	dozen cherry tomatoes
4	small bok choy, cut in half lengthwise
3 to 4	red bell peppers, cut in half lengthwise
3 to 4	ears of corn, silks removed, husks attached

PARSLEY VINAIGRETTE

2	shallots, minced
½	cup white wine vinegar
4	garlic cloves, minced
⅛	teaspoon kosher (coarse) salt
⅛	teaspoon freshly ground pepper
¾	cup minced Italian parsley
3	tablespoons fresh lemon juice
1	cup olive oil

Serves 6.
1¾ cups Vinaigrette.
Preparation time: 1 hour.
Ready to serve: 1 hour, 30 minutes.

1 Heat grill.

2 Using paring knife, make several tiny slits into each sausage. Place sausages in large pot of boiling water; poach 3 to 4 minutes. Drain thoroughly and pat dry; set aside.

3 Place potatoes in medium saucepan; add enough water to cover, plus 2 inches. Add 3 tablespoons salt; bring to a boil over high heat. Reduce heat to medium; simmer about 7 minutes or until potatoes are about crisp tender. Drain and rinse in cool water; drain again.

4 Thread 3 potatoes onto each of 4 skewers; set aside. Brush onions with olive oil; set aside. Brush cut sides of eggplant and zucchini with olive oil; season with salt and pepper, then set aside. Thread 3 mushrooms onto each of 4 skewers; set aside. Thread 6 tomatoes onto each of 4 skewers; set aside. Brush cut sides of bok choy with olive oil; season with salt and pepper.

5 Place potato, mushroom and tomato skewers on gas grill directly over medium heat or on charcoal grill 4 to 6 inches from medium coals. Cook 6 to 8 minutes or until vegetables are tender; remove to serving platter and cover to keep warm. Place onions on grill slightly off center from heat; cook 10 to 12 minutes or until slightly charred and softened. Add eggplant, zucchini, bell peppers, corn and bok choy; turn frequently to avoid burning. Cook 10 to 12 minutes or until vegetables are crisp tender.

6 Remove vegetables from grill. Remove corn husks and break corn in half. Cut peppers into

lengthwise strips. Cover cooked vegetables to keep warm.

7 Cut sausages into thirds, making diagonal slices, and pile them in center of large serving platter. Arrange vegetables around sausages.

8 For Parsley Vinaigrette: In medium bowl, combine shallots and vinegar; let stand several minutes to blend flavors. Add garlic, salt and pepper. Stir in parsley and lemon juice. Whisk in olive oil. Spoon a little of the vinaigrette over each sausage. Serve immediately with any remaining vinaigrette on the side.

GARLIC LAMB KABOBS

These savory kabobs are wonderful served on top of steamed rice with a splash of fresh lemon juice.

1	garlic bulb, cloves separated, peeled
2	tablespoons kosher (coarse) salt
	Grated peel of 1 lemon
2	teaspoons freshly ground black pepper
¼	teaspoon crushed red pepper
3 to 4	tablespoons olive oil
4 lb.	lamb stew meat, trimmed
1	bunch cilantro, rinsed, dried, stems trimmed
4	lemon wedges

Serves 4.
Preparation time: 25 minutes.
Ready to serve: 8 hours, 45 minutes.

1 In mortar, grind garlic and salt until garlic is nearly liquefied. Add lemon peel, black and red pepper; mix. Stir in olive oil until thick paste forms; set aside.

2 Place lamb into medium bowl. Spoon garlic paste over lamb. Stir lamb until it's evenly coated with garlic mixture. Cover and refrigerate 6 to 8 hours.

3 Heat oven to 400°F. Thread lamb onto skewers*; arrange skewers on roasting rack over baking sheet. Bake, turning 2 or 3 times, until kabobs are medium rare, about 20 minutes.

4 Spread cilantro over clean serving platter. Arrange kabobs on top. Garnish with lemon wedges; serve immediately.

TIP* 12 (12-inch) bamboo skewers, soaked in water for at least 30 minutes.

ROASTED CHICKEN WITH OLIVE-POLENTA STUFFING

If you have the time, brine your chicken; it will improve the flavor and ensure that it remains moist. To brine, mix ¾ cup kosher salt and 1 gallon water. Put rinsed chicken into a large container, pour the brine over it, refrigerate and let rest 1 hour. Drain the chicken and pat dry.

POLENTA

2	teaspoons kosher (coarse) salt
½	cup coarse-ground polenta
2	teaspoons butter
½	cup pitted ripe olives, minced
⅛	teaspoon freshly ground pepper

STUFFING

1	tablespoon olive oil
2	oz. diced pancetta
½	cup pitted ripe olives of choice, chopped
3	tablespoons minced Italian parsley
1	tablespoon fresh thyme
1	tablespoon fresh oregano
	Peel of 1 lemon, grated
⅛	teaspoon kosher (coarse) salt
⅛	teaspoon freshly ground pepper

CHICKEN

1	large range chicken, about 4½ lb.

Serves 4.
Preparation time: 1 hour.
Ready to serve: 2 hours, 30 minutes.

1 For Polenta: Place 2½ cups water in medium saucepan. Add salt; bring to a boil over medium-high heat. Using whisk, stir polenta vigorously into water. Reduce heat to medium; continue to stir until polenta thickens. (If you find lumps, use a wooden spoon to press lumps against side of pot.)

2 Continue stirring polenta until it is very thick and pulls away from sides of pot. (Taste to be sure grains of polenta are tender; it will take 15 to 60 minutes, the longer time for certain types of cornmeal that do not become tender quickly.) During last 5 minutes of cooking, stir in butter and olives.

Season with pepper. Remove from heat; let sit 5 minutes.

3 Meanwhile, rinse 8-inch square pan in cool water; shake out excess water but do not dry. Pour polenta into pan; shake to evenly distribute.

4 Brush piece of parchment paper lightly with olive oil. Set paper, olive oil-side down, on top of hot polenta. Let rest at room temperature 30 minutes. Cover pan with plastic wrap; refrigerate at least 2 hours or overnight.

5 For Stuffing: Cut polenta into 1-inch cubes. In large skillet, heat 1 tablespoon olive oil over medium-high heat until hot. Add polenta; fry until polenta loses its raw color, about 6 to 8 minutes. In large bowl, combine fried polenta, pancetta, olives, parsley, thyme, oregano, lemon peel, salt and pepper. Set aside.

6 Heat oven to 425°F.

7 Rinse chicken under cool water, pat dry; let rest, central cavity down, about 10 minutes.

8 Season inside of chicken with salt and pepper. Fill cavity with stuffing; secure wings and legs of chicken with twine. Season outside of chicken with salt and pepper. Bake 40 minutes.

9 Reduce oven temperature to 375°F. Brush chicken with olive oil; cook about 1 hour, 45 minutes or until juices run clear when thickest part of thigh is cut. Remove chicken from oven; cover loosely. Let rest 10 minutes. Remove and discard twine. Using large spoon, scoop out stuffing onto serving platter. Carve chicken; arrange meat around stuffing and serve immediately.

PORK TENDERLOIN WITH MEDJOOL DATE BUTTER

Medjool dates from California are rich and sweet — perfect in the fall, when summer's fruits are no longer available. These dates are particularly wonderful with pork.

TENDERLOINS

	Peel of 2 oranges, minced
⅛	teaspoon salt
	Dash of sugar
⅛	teaspoon freshly ground pepper
2	pork tenderloins, about 1½ lb. each

DATE BUTTER

6	oz. unsalted butter, softened
5	Medjool dates, pitted, diced
	Peel of 1 orange, grated
⅛	teaspoon freshly ground pepper
¾	teaspoon sugar
½	teaspoon kosher (coarse) salt
2	tablespoons Italian parsley, minced
	Medjool dates, for garnish

Serves 4.

Preparation time: 25 minutes.
Ready to serve: 13 hours, 25 minutes.

1 In small bowl, combine orange peel, salt, sugar and pepper. Rub orange mixture over surface of pork. Set tenderloins on plate, cover with parchment paper; refrigerate several hours or overnight.

2 For Date Butter: In blender or food processor, combine butter, dates, orange peel, pepper, sugar and salt; pulse until mixture is smooth. Line work surface with parchment paper. Transfer date butter to paper. Shape butter into log about 1¼ inches in diameter; roll paper around butter. Twist ends, roll package in plastic wrap; refrigerate at least 2 hours, or up to 5 days. (Date butter may be frozen for 3 weeks.)

3 Heat oven to 375°F. Set tenderloins on rack over roasting pan; bake, turning once, 20 minutes or until meat reaches an internal temperature of 165°F. Transfer to work surface. Cover loosely with aluminum foil; let rest 5 minutes.

4 Meanwhile, cut date butter into ¼-inch-thick slices. In small pot, melt half of the butter over medium heat. Brush butter over tenderloins. Cut tenderloins into thin, diagonal slices. Arrange on individual plates. Top each portion with remaining date butter slices. Sprinkle parsley over each portion. Garnish with dates; serve immediately.

*P*opcorn is a treat enjoyed by all ages. These colorful bags of popcorn seeds make wonderful gifts for your guests to bring home. Create quick and easy decorative name tags using craft punches. You can also fill the bags with fancy nuts or different layers of dried fruit befitting of autumn.

MATERIALS AND TOOLS

- ❏ RED AND YELLOW POPCORN SEEDS
- ❏ SMALL CLEAR BAGS
- ❏ VELLUM
- ❏ RAFFIA
- ❏ CLEAR DOUBLE SIDED TAPE
- ❏ FINE GOLD METALLIC MARKER
- ❏ EXTRA-FINE GOLD METALLIC MARKER
- ❏ SUPER JUMBO MAPLE LEAF CRAFT PUNCH
- ❏ MINI OAK LEAF CRAFT PUNCH
- ❏ ⅛-INCH HOLE PUNCH
- ❏ SCISSORS
- ❏ PENCIL

DIRECTIONS

1 Punch a maple leaf out of vellum paper. Punch a mini oak leaf onto the maple leaf. Leave enough room to write the name.

2 Outline the edge of the maple leaf by rubbing the edge of the paper with a fine gold marker. Write the name with an extra-fine gold marker.

3 Fill a bag with mixed popcorn seeds. Tie a raffia bow around the bag. Put a small piece of clear double-sided tape on the back of the leaf and adhere it to the bag.

BAKED SWEET POTATOES WITH WALNUT AND PARSLEY BUTTER

Sweet potatoes are so intensely sweet that they need something savory and salty, such as this butter, to signal that this is not dessert.

POTATOES

4	small-medium sweet potatoes

WALNUT AND PARSLEY BUTTER

1	garlic clove, crushed
2	tablespoons chopped toasted walnuts
6	tablespoons unsalted butter, softened
2	tablespoons minced Italian parsley
1/8	teaspoon kosher (coarse) salt
1/8	teaspoon freshly ground pepper

Serves 4.
Preparation time: 10 minutes.
Ready to serve: 40 to 70 minutes.

1 Heat oven to 400°F. Wash sweet potatoes, dry and pierce each one in several places. Set potatoes on wire rack set over baking sheet. Bake until tender, about 30 to 60 minutes, depending on size.

2 Meanwhile, prepare Walnut and Parsley Butter: In mortar with pestle, crush garlic into paste. Add walnuts; crush with garlic. Transfer mixture to small bowl. Mix in butter. Add parsley, salt and pepper; cover and set aside.

3 Make one small, lengthwise slit on top of each potato. Spoon generous tablespoon of the butter mixture into each potato. Season with pepper and serve immediately.

POLENTA TARAGNA WITH GARLIC CHARD

Polenta with buckwheat flour, known in Italy as Polenta Taragna, *has an earthiness to it that is quite delicious and particularly wonderful in the fall, when it is so good with a variety of seasonal vegetables, especially the winter squashes and fall greens.*

POLENTA TARAGNA

6	cups water
1	tablespoon kosher (coarse) salt
1	cup coarse-ground polenta
2	tablespoons buckwheat flour

GARLIC CHARD

1	bunch (about 1¼ lb.) Swiss chard, stems removed
1	tablespoon olive oil
2	garlic cloves, pressed
⅛	teaspoon salt
⅛	teaspoon freshly ground pepper
4	tablespoons butter
4	oz. Italian Taleggio or California TelemeJack cheese, diced

Serves 4.
Preparation time: 25 minutes.
Ready to serve: 40 minutes.

1 In large heavy pot, bring 6 cups water to a rolling boil over high heat. Remove 2 cups of the water into small saucepan and set over low heat.

2 In small bowl, combine salt, polenta and buckwheat flour. Stir 4 cups water into large pot rapidly with whisk; pour polenta mixture in steady, thin stream, stirring vigorously to prevent formation of lumps. When mixture returns to a boil, reduce heat to low and simmer until polenta begins to thicken. With wooden spoon, continue to stir, pressing any lumps against side of pot to break them up. Add reserved water, ¼ cup at a time, as necessary to keep polenta from becoming too thick.

3 Meanwhile, prepare Garlic Chard: Stack leaves and cut them into 1-inch-wide crosswise strips. In wok or large skillet, heat olive oil over medium heat until hot. Add garlic; cook about 15 seconds or until fragrant. Add chard and 3 tablespoons of water to wok; cook, stirring continuously, until chard is limp and water has evaporated. Season with salt and pepper, set aside, covered.

4 Shortly before polenta is completely tender, stir in butter and cheese. Remove from heat; let rest 5 minutes. Top with chard mixture and serve.

GREEN BEANS AND GEMELLI WITH CHERRY TOMATOES

Gemelli is a hollow pasta cut into about 4-inch lengths and then folded and twisted around itself. It is the ideal size and texture to serve with green beans, though any medium-length pasta will do. Be sure to test the beans before taking them out of their cooking water; they should be tender, not al dente.

1	tablespoon kosher (coarse) salt
½	lb. French green beans
½	lb. gemelli
3	tablespoons extra-virgin olive oil
1	small shallot, minced
2	garlic cloves, minced
⅛	teaspoon freshly ground pepper
2	cups cherry tomatoes, halved
1	teaspoon minced fresh tarragon
¼	cup (1 oz.) freshly grated Parmigiano-Reggiano cheese

Serves 4.
Preparation time: 20 minutes.
Ready to serve: 30 minutes.

1 Fill large pot half full with water. Add salt; bring water to a boil over high heat. When water comes to a rolling boil, add beans and cook 3 minutes. Remove beans, shaking off excess water. Set beans aside; keep warm. Fill large pot with water; bring to a boil over high heat. Add pasta; cook until tender. Drain but do not rinse.

2 Meanwhile, heat olive oil in large sauté pan over medium-low heat until hot. Add shallots and garlic; cook 2 minutes. Season with pepper. Add tomatoes; cook, stirring frequently, until heated through. Add tarragon and cooked green beans; remove from heat.

3 Put pasta in large bowl. Add green beans and tomato mixture; toss together gently. Sprinkle grated cheese over; serve immediately.

MASHED POTATOES WITH CHIVES AND BACON

If you have been plagued by lumpy mashed potatoes, you'll be very pleased with the results when you use a potato ricer or a food mill, as suggested here.

2	lb. Yukon Gold potatoes, coarsely chopped
1	tablespoon kosher (coarse) salt
4	thick slices bacon, cooked, cut into 1-inch pieces
¾	cup hot half-and-half
3	tablespoons butter, softened
3	tablespoons fresh minced chives
⅛	teaspoon freshly ground pepper

Serves 4.

Preparation time: 15 minutes.

Ready to serve: 40 minutes.

1 Put potatoes in medium saucepan. Cover potatoes with water; add salt. Bring to a boil over high heat; reduce heat to medium-low, then simmer until potatoes are tender when pierced with fork, about 20 to 25 minutes. Drain thoroughly.

2 Press potatoes through potato ricer or food mill into medium bowl. Add half-and-half, crumbled bacon, butter, chives and pepper; mix until smooth. Serve immediately.

*F*ancy candlesticks set the tone for a special dinner. Personalize them with a stamped word, your initial or a decorative design. These candlesticks will also make a wonderful gift to give to a host. Wax glue is easier to use than melting real wax. Try gold ink instead of clear embossing ink as a release to create a gilded effect. The leaves give this decoration and autumn feel.

MATERIALS AND TOOLS

- ❑ CANDLESTICKS
- ❑ SKELETONIZED LEAVES
- ❑ WAX GLUE STICKS
- ❑ RELEASE PAPER
- ❑ CLEAR EMBOSSING INK
- ❑ STAMP
- ❑ LOW-TEMPERATURE GLUE GUN

DIRECTIONS

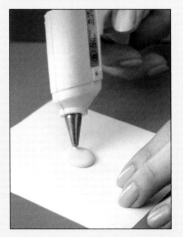

1 Insert a wax glue stick into the glue gun and let it heat up. Press a mound of wax glue onto the release paper. Let it set 15 seconds.

2 Coat the stamp with clear embossing ink, which acts as a releasing agent. Stamp the wax glue and let it harden about 30 seconds before removing the stamp.

3 Peel off the imprinted seal and adhere a few skeletonized leaves to the back with low-temperature hot glue. Apply more to the back and place it onto the candle.

PARSLEY COUSCOUS WITH HARISSA

Although you can make couscous according to the package directions, it will be much better if you steam it, as suggested in this recipe.

HARISSA

1½	oz. dried chiles, such as anchos
5	garlic cloves, crushed
1	tablespoon ground cumin
1	teaspoon ground coriander seeds
1	teaspoon ground caraway seeds
2	teaspoons kosher (coarse) salt
½	cup olive oil
½	cup fresh-squeezed lemon juice

COUSCOUS

1¾	cup water
1	cup couscous
¼	cup minced cilantro
¼	cup minced Italian parsley

Serves 4.
Preparation time: 25 minutes.
Ready to serve: 45 minutes.

1 For Harissa: Using blender, food processor or heavy molca jete (Mexican mortar and pestle), grind chiles, garlic, cumin, coriander, caraway and salt until thick paste forms. Stir in olive oil and lemon juice. Drizzle with water to thin if necessary; set aside.

2 For Couscous: In medium bowl, pour ¾ cup of the water over couscous. Let sit until water is absorbed, about 10 minutes. Put couscous into strainer with small enough holes to contain it; set in large pot filled with about 3 inches of water. Wrap damp towel around space between colander and pot; set over high heat, uncovered, 10 minutes or until steam is rising from couscous.

3 Remove couscous from heat. Set colander on work surface; drizzle remaining cup of water over couscous while stirring it with fork. Return colander to pot; steam again until couscous is about 3 times its original size.

4 Put couscous in large serving bowl. Add half of the cilantro and half of the Italian parsley; fluff with fork. Heat harissa. Remove from heat; stir remaining cilantro and parsley into heated harissa. Spoon some of the harissa over the couscous. Serve immediately with remaining harissa. Harissa will keep, covered, in the refrigerator up to 1 week.

POACHED PEARS WITH POMEGRANATES AND CREME FRAICHE

Pears and pomegranates are two of fall's most beloved treasures. Here they are served together in a simple yet satisfying dessert.

3	cups light-bodied red wine (Beaujolais)
2	cups sugar
1	cinnamon stick
4 to 6	small Anjou or Comice pears, peeled
¼	cup crème fraîche
	Seeds from 1 pomegranate

Serves 4.
Preparation time: 10 minutes.
Ready to serve: 40 minutes.

1 In large saucepan, bring wine and sugar to a boil over medium heat. Reduce heat to low; stir until sugar is dissolved. Add cinnamon stick and set pears in syrup; add enough water to cover pears. Simmer until pears are tender when pierced, about 15 minutes. They should not be mushy.

2 With slotted spoon, transfer pears to individual large soup bowls. Increase heat to high; simmer until poaching liquid is reduce by two-thirds, about 10 minutes. Stir in crème fraîche.

3 Ladle sauce over pears. Garnish with pomegranate seeds; serve immediately.

THIN-CRUSTED APPLE TART

The year's first apples, the fragile and highly coveted Gravensteins, ripen in July; by fall, there are dozens of other varieties available, especially if you shop at farm stands or farmers' markets. Make this French-inspired tart using whatever apples you prefer. If you keep a supply of apples in a cool place, you'll be able to make this tart not only in the fall, but throughout the winter too. (This tart is also excellent made with pears, though you should omit the sugar and spices.)

1	cup all-purpose flour
½	teaspoon plus ⅛ teaspoon kosher (coarse) salt
½	cup (1 stick) unsalted butter, cut into pieces, chilled
3	tablespoons ice water
	Juice of 1 lemon
3 to 4	sweet-tart apples
3	tablespoons unsalted butter, melted
3	tablespoons sugar
1	teaspoon ground cinnamon
⅛	teaspoon ground cloves
⅛	teaspoon ground nutmeg
3	tablespoons apple jelly, warmed

Serves 6 to 8.

Preparation time: 25 minutes.
Ready to serve: 1 hour, 5 minutes.

1 In large bowl, combine flour and ½ teaspoon of salt. With pastry blender or two forks, cut butter into flour until it resembles coarse crumbs. Add ice water; mix.

2 Shape dough into ball and cover with plastic wrap; refrigerate 1 hour.

3 Fill medium bowl half full with water; add lemon juice. Peel apples and cut each apple into ⅛-inch-thick slices. Place apples in water.

4 Heat oven to 375°F. Sprinkle work surface generously with flour. Roll out dough to form 11-inch round, about ⅛ inch thick. Transfer to nonstick baking sheet. Turn in outer edge to form ½-inch rim. Use tines of fork to press rim into place. Prick in several places.

5 Drain apples, shaking them vigorously to remove excess water; dry. Arrange one circle of overlapping apple slices at far edge of dough. Repeat with remaining apple slices, working all the way into center. Brush apples and outer rim of dough with melted butter.

6 In small bowl, combine sugar, cinnamon, cloves, nutmeg and remaining ⅛ teaspoon of salt. Sprinkle sugar mixture over apples. Bake 40 to 45 minutes or until apples are tender and crust is golden brown. Remove tart from oven to wire rack; cool 5 minutes. Remove tart to serving plate; brush with warmed jelly. Cut into wedges; serve immediately.

GRILLED BANANAS WITH ICE CREAM AND CHOCOLATE SAUCE

Bananas develop a wonderful intensity when they are grilled; they are nearly as good served over rice pudding as they are with ice cream.

6	firm-ripe bananas, peeled, cut in half lengthwise then crosswise
	Juice of 2 limes
2	tablespoons packed brown sugar
¼	teaspoon kosher (coarse) salt
4	oz. good-quality bittersweet chocolate
3	tablespoons cream or half-and-half
1	pint coconut ice cream
¼	cup unsweetened dried coconut, toasted

Serves 4.

Preparation time: 15 minutes.
Ready to serve: 45 minutes.

1 Heat grill.

2 Prepare small double boiler over medium-low heat.

3 Place cut bananas in wide, shallow bowl.

4 In small bowl, combine lime juice, brown sugar and salt. Brush each banana piece with lime juice mixture.

5 Place bananas on grill 4 to 6 inches from medium coals; cook, turning frequently, 3 to 4 minutes or until they are evenly marked and heated through. Transfer bananas to serving platter; cover.

6 In double boiler, heat chocolate until melted. Gently stir in cream. Remove from heat.

7 Place generous scoops of ice cream in individual dessert bowls; top with several pieces of grilled banana and chocolate sauce. Sprinkle with toasted coconut. Serve immediately.

GINGER PUMPKIN ICE CREAM

It can be hard to find good pumpkin ice cream; most of it tastes like frozen pumpkin pie. This special ice cream is, however, very easy to make at home if you have an ice-cream maker. This cool treat is wonderful during an Indian summer heat wave.

ICE CREAM

2	cups heavy cream
6	quarter-size slices fresh ginger
2	teaspoons freshly ground pepper
1	cinnamon stick
1	(2-inch piece) vanilla bean
6	egg yolks
1	cup granulated sugar
½	teaspoon kosher (coarse) salt
2	cups baked, pureed, strained sugar pumpkin*
3	tablespoons crystallized ginger, finely diced
4	gingersnap cookies
4	small sprigs of mint, for garnish

Serves 4.
Preparation time: 45 minutes.
Ready to serve: 13 hours, 30 minutes.

1 Prepare double boiler.

2 In medium saucepan, heat cream over medium heat. Just before it boils, remove saucepan from heat. Stir in ginger, pepper, cinnamon and vanilla; cover. Steep mixture 30 minutes; strain.

3 In double boiler, mix together egg yolks, sugar and salt until creamy but not foamy. Set over slowly simmering water; stir until mixture thickens. Whisk in pumpkin and ginger mixture. Pour through strainer into bowl; cover and refrigerate overnight.

4 Remove chilled custard from refrigerator; stir in crystallized ginger. Freeze in ice-cream maker according to the manufacturer's instructions. Garnish with gingersnaps and mint; serve immediately.

TIP* Do not use a jack-o-lantern pumpkin for this recipe; they are best for carving. Sugar pumpkins are heavy, deep orange pumpkins, generally used for pie, and are the best ones to use in this recipe, though almost any dense winter squash will work. To cook, cut into large pieces, set on a roasting rack over a baking sheet, and bake at 325°F until very tender, about 40 to 45 minutes.

FALL FRUIT COBBLER

Make this cobbler as long as you have fruit that is in season; a cobbler can never be better than the fruit that goes into it.

4	cups fall fruit*
1	tablespoon fresh lemon juice
⅓ to ½	cup sugar
2	tablespoons brandy
1	teaspoon vanilla
2	tablespoons instant tapioca
¾	cup all-purpose flour
1	teaspoon salt
½	teaspoon baking power
1	tablespoon sugar
2	tablespoons butter, chilled, cut into small pieces
½	cup heavy cream

Serves 6.
Preparation time: 25 minutes.
Ready to serve: 1 hour.

1 Heat oven to 350°F.

2 In large bowl, toss fruit, lemon juice and ⅓ cup sugar. In small bowl, mix together brandy, vanilla and tapioca. Place fruit in 3-quart casserole. Pour brandy mixture over fruit; toss.

3 In medium mixing bowl, combine flour, salt, baking powder and sugar. With pastry blender or two forks, cut in butter until mixture forms coarse crumbs. Pour in cream. Stir until mixture forms a dough; knead once or twice. Place dough on floured work surface; roll dough until it is one-half inch thick and cut into 2-inch shapes such as maple leaves, stars, hearts or circles.

4 Cover fruit with pastry shapes. Bake until golden brown and fruit is thickened and bubbly, about 35 to 40 minutes. Remove from oven; cool slightly. Serve warm.

TIP* I use a mixture of the season's fruit such as peaches, blackberries and raspberries. If you have good nectarines, you can use them in this recipe. Apples also work great. Be sure to taste the fruit and add more sugar if necessary.

MAPLE LEAF
DECORATED BREAD BASKET

*D*ecorate your bread basket with dried fall leaves. Collect and press small leaves during the fall, or purchase them at the craft store. Clear acrylic spray sealant protects the delicate leaves with a hard glossy coating. You could also use these attractive leaves to decorate place cards.

MATERIALS AND TOOLS

- ❑ BREAD BASKET
- ❑ PRESSED LEAVES
- ❑ CLEAR ACRYLIC SPRAY SEALANT
- ❑ PARCHMENT PAPER
- ❑ HOT GLUE
- ❑ HOT-GLUE GUN

DIRECTIONS

1 Lay the leaves onto parchment paper and spray them with clear acrylic spray sealant. Let them dry.

2 Turn the leaves over and spray the other side. Repeat at least four times on each side. Let them dry completely.

3 Hot-glue the leaves onto the basket.

winter HOLIDAYS

Christmas

Hanukkah

New Year's Day

President's Day

Valentine's Day

St. Patrick's Day

Birthday

Anniversary

Winter Solstice

Bowl Party

Kwanzaa

Ground Hog Day

Leap Year

Mardi Gras

CHESTNUT GNOCCHI WITH POPPY SEED BROWNED BUTTER

Start a traditional Italian Christmas with gnocchi (NYO-key). Usually little potato dumplings, here they get a Christmas twist with canned chestnuts. Buy them in glass jars so you can see if they're fresh. They should 1) look pale beige or bright brown, not dusty or wooden; 2) still be whole, not crushed; and 3) look moist, not desiccated.

1	(10-oz.) can chestnuts, drained
½	cup all-purpose flour, plus additional for the fork
1	large egg yolk
¼	teaspoon salt
3	tablespoons unsalted butter, at room temperature
½	teaspoon poppy seeds
¼	teaspoon grated nutmeg

6 servings.
Preparation time: 30 minutes.
Ready to serve: 35 minutes.

1 Place chestnuts in fine-mesh strainer. Using back of wooden spoon, push through mesh sieve and into large bowl. Alternatively, place in potato ricer and rice into large bowl. Mix in flour, just until moistened; then mix in egg yolk and salt. Use your hands to knead into a dough, then pull off small balls, about the size of a whole almond, making about 36 balls. Roll each between your palms until slightly flattened.

2 Hold fork's tines against your work surface with fork's handle toward you, so that the back of the tines curve toward you. Dust with flour, then roll balls up the tines, pressing gently to form shallow grooves.

3 Bring large pot of salted water to a boil. Add gnocchi; boil until tender, about 3 minutes. Drain.

4 In large skillet or sauté pan, melt butter over medium heat until foam subsides and butter turns pale brown. Add poppy seeds and nutmeg; stir until fragrant, about 10 seconds. Add cooked gnocchi; sauté 30 seconds. Serve at once.

CREAMY CARROT AND WALNUT SOUP

This soup is thickened with pureed carrots and ground walnuts. Your guests will probably swear there's cream in it, but you can tell them it's actually a healthy alternative to cream soups — a new start for the year. Besides, carrots are so sweet, they're the perfect symbol to wish us all a sweet new year!

2	tablespoons unsalted butter
2	medium shallots, chopped
2	teaspoons curry powder*
1	tablespoon all-purpose flour
3	cups chicken stock
1	(1-lb.) bag peeled baby carrots
⅔	cup walnut pieces, toasted
½	teaspoon salt
¼	teaspoon freshly ground pepper

6 servings.
Preparation time: 5 minutes.
Ready to serve: 1 hour, 5 minutes.

1 In large saucepan, melt butter over medium heat. Add shallots; cook, stirring often, about 2 minutes. Sprinkle in curry powder and flour; stir well, then cook 2 minutes or until flour browns slightly, stirring constantly.

2 Whisk in stock in thin, steady stream; continue whisking and cooking until mixture thickens, about 1 minute. Add carrots and walnut pieces; cover, then reduce heat to low and simmer until carrots are quite soft, about 45 minutes.

3 Transfer soup to large blender. Puree until smooth, scraping down sides of bowl with wooden spoon as necessary. Work in batches if necessary. Return to large saucepan set over medium heat. Bring to simmer, stirring often to prevent ground walnuts from scorching. Cook and stir 5 minutes to blend flavors. Season with salt and pepper, then serve.

TIP* Curry powder is actually a blend of spices. Some powders are quite bland because of all the turmeric; others, fiery because of all the cayenne. In any case, the interaction among the spices' oils can cause curry powder to lose its flavor quickly, rendering any variety dusty and slightly tangy. Store curry powder in a dry, dark and cool place for no more than 3 months.

BORSCHT WITH A FORK

Borscht is a beet soup spiked with horseradish, served hot or cold in Jewish delicatessens. For a Hanukkah or other holiday meal, it becomes a roasted beet starter, dressed with a creamy, spicy horseradish dressing. Let the beet mixture stand in the refrigerator for several hours to ripen and develop the flavors.

8	medium beets, peeled
¼	cup chopped fresh dill
2	tablespoons olive oil or vegetable oil
2	teaspoons red wine vinegar
1	teaspoon salt
½	teaspoon freshly ground pepper
¾	cup sour cream (regular, low-fat or nonfat)
2	tablespoons prepared white horseradish

6 servings.
Preparation time: 10 minutes.
Ready to serve: 3 hours, 55 minutes.

1 Heat oven to 400°F. Wrap beets tightly in aluminum foil; bake until tender, about 1 hour. Carefully unwrap; save any liquid in foil packet. Cool beets, then shred with large holes of box grater. Place grated beets in large bowl; stir in any liquid from foil packet. Stir in dill, oil, vinegar, salt and pepper.

2 In small bowl, mix sour cream and horseradish until smooth. Cover both bowls and place in refrigerator until chilled, at least 2 hours, or up to 24 hours.

3 To serve, mound beet mixture on each plate; top with sour cream dressing.

BROCCOLI SOUP

One of our more recent Presidents may have had an issue with broccoli, but even he learned to like it. So on this President's Day, we salute learning to like new things. And who wouldn't like a velvety, soft, comforting broccoli soup, rich and fresh, topped with grated cheese?

4	tablespoons (¼ cup) unsalted butter
4	medium onions, thinly sliced (about 4 cups)
3	cups chicken stock
2	large heads broccoli (about 1½ lb. total weight), broken into florets, the stalks thinly sliced
2	teaspoons chopped fresh thyme or 1 teaspoon dried
½	teaspoon salt
½	teaspoon freshly ground pepper
¾	cup grated Gruyère cheese

6 servings.
Preparation time: 10 minutes.
Ready to serve: 1 hour, 35 minutes.

1 In large saucepan, melt butter over low heat. The moment foam appears, add onion slices; cook 20 minutes, stirring often. If onion browns, reduce heat further. After 20 minutes, cover pan and cook an additional 25 minutes, stirring frequently, until onions are soft and sweet.

2 Raise heat to medium-high. Pour in stock and stir in broccoli and thyme; bring to a simmer. Cover and reduce heat to low; simmer 1 hour or until broccoli is very soft.

3 Stir to break broccoli into small pieces, then season with salt and pepper. Divide soup evenly into 6 bowls. Top each with 2 tablespoons grated cheese. Serve immediately.

Place a small gift box filled with candy, chocolate or a novelty item at each place setting. These attractive boxes only need a ribbon to finish them. The translucent paper hints at what is inside. Also try making gift boxes out of clear heavyweight acetate for a unique presentation.

MATERIALS AND TOOLS

- ❏ HEAVYWEIGHT VELLUM
- ❏ SMALL BOX (TO USE AS A PATTERN)
- ❏ RIBBON
- ❏ DOUBLE-STICK TAPE
- ❏ BONE FOLDER
- ❏ XACTO KNIFE (CRAFT KNIFE)
- ❏ SCISSORS
- ❏ RULER
- ❏ PENCIL

DIRECTIONS

1 Disassemble a small box to use as a pattern. Outline the box with pencil onto vellum paper.

2 Cut the pattern using scissors. Using an Xacto knife and a ruler as a guide, score the edges of the box.

3 Fold the edges using a bone folder for a crisper fold. Apply double-stick tape to the flaps; cut any excess tape. Assemble the box. Place a gift inside. Tie a ribbon around the box and attach a name tag as a place card, if desired.

SMOKED OYSTER CANAPES

Oysters have long been touted as an aphrodisiac, and dates were once forbidden in some Middle Eastern cultures because of proclivities they were said to foster among the young. Together, and wrapped in paper-thin slices of prosciutto (a smoked ham from Italy, the land of romance), they make a good start to any Valentine's Day.

18	large pitted dates
1	(3.7-oz.) can smoked oysters (contains about 18 smoked oysters)
4	oz. prosciutto, sliced paper thin*
18	toothpicks

6 servings.
Preparation time: 15 minutes.
Ready to serve: 15 minutes.

1 Using sharp paring knife, make slit-like pockets in dates. Slip one oyster into each pocket. (It may not fit all the way inside.) Wrap stuffed date with 1 (4- to 6-inch) prosciutto strip; secure with toothpick. Repeat to create 18 canapés. Serve immediately.

TIP* Ask your butcher or the deli clerk to slice the prosciutto as thinly as possible. Have him or her then layer the slices between strips of parchment paper so they don't dry out before use.

ROASTED POTATO SALAD

Here's a hearty salad, perfect for a winter night. It's made by scooping the potatoes into balls using a melon baller, thereby producing little round potato orbs. Yes, there's some waste, but the results are fantastic: airy potato balls, crunchy outside and fluffy inside.

4	large Russet potatoes, peeled (about 1 lb.)
6	tablespoons olive oil
1	teaspoon kosher (coarse) salt
½	teaspoon freshly ground pepper
5	large shallots, peeled and quartered
½	cup chopped fresh parsley
1	rib celery, chopped
1	red bell pepper, cored, seeded, and chopped
1½	teaspoons cider vinegar

6 servings.
Preparation time: 15 minutes.
Ready to serve: 90 minutes.

1 Heat oven to 500°F. Use 1 ³⁄₁₆-inch melon baller to cut balls out of potato flesh. Place potatoes' balls in large bowl; toss with oil, salt and pepper. Pour into large baking dish. Bake 45 minutes, stirring occasionally.

2 Stir shallots and parsley into pan; immediately reduce oven temperature to 450°F. Bake an additional 30 minutes or until all is browned and crisp.

3 Transfer to serving bowl. Toss with celery, bell pepper and cider vinegar. Let stand 5 minutes to absorb flavors, then serve.

FRESH START SALAD

Quinoa has been labeled a "supergrain" by the World Health Organization. No wonder. This South American staple is loaded with protein, and not the partial proteins of other grains, but a full chain of all eight amino acids. Quinoa is also low in saturated fat; when cooked, the grains look like beige poppy seeds surrounded by a translucent halo.

⅔	cup quinoa
1⅓	cups water
½	teaspoon salt
½	teaspoon freshly ground pepper
1	tablespoons Champagne vinegar or white wine vinegar
2	teaspoons lime juice
5	tablespoons olive oil
2	small avocados, peeled, pitted and diced
1	small red onion, thinly sliced
1	cup orange supremes, or orange segments (from about 2 medium oranges) or 1 (5-oz.) can orange segments, drained
2	tablespoons toasted sliced almonds
1	tablespoons chopped fresh parsley

6 servings.
Preparation time: 10 minutes.
Ready to serve: 30 minutes.

1 In medium saucepan, bring water to a boil over medium-high heat. Add quinoa; cover and reduce heat to low. Simmer 10 minutes. Fluff with fork; cover again and let stand off heat 5 minutes. Transfer to serving bowl; season with salt and pepper.

2 In small bowl, whisk vinegar and lime juice. Whisk in oil in steady, thin stream until emulsified. Set aside.

3 Stir avocados, red onion, orange segments, almonds and parsley into quinoa. Pour on dressing; toss again and serve.

TRICOLORI SALAD

Long a staple of Italian restaurants, this salad of three colors (red, white, and green, like the Italian flag) here gets a new twist with an apricot vinaigrette. Its sweet tanginess nicely balances greens' bitterness.

1	(6-oz.) can apricot halves, drained
2	tablespoons cider vinegar
¼	teaspoon salt, or to taste
¼	teaspoon freshly ground pepper
5	tablespoons olive oil, preferably extra-virgin olive oil
2	heads Belgian endive (about 4 oz. each)*
2	medium heads radicchio (about 5 oz. each)
2	cups arugula leaves, washed, dried, and roughly chopped

6 servings.
Preparation time: 5 minutes.
Ready to serve: 15 minutes.

1 Place apricot halves, vinegar, salt and pepper in blender or food processor fitted with chopping blade; pulse four or five times, until smooth, then scrape down sides of bowl. With blades running, drizzle in oil, scraping sides as necessary. Blend or process until smooth and emulsified. The dressing can be made in advance; store, covered, in refrigerator up to 3 days — bring to room temperature and whisk to incorporate any oil before using.

2 Cut tough bottom ends off endives, then pry open leaves and remove any center ones with frizzled tops. Chop remaining leaves into 1-inch segments; place in serving bowl. Core radicchio and roughly chop; place in serving bowl as well. Add chopped arugula leaves; toss well.

3 Pour dressing over greens. Toss well and serve.

TIP* Belgian endive is a fairly bitter green. To control its bitterness, look at the color gradient in the leaves. More green and less white means a less bitter green. Avoid Belgian endive spears with a sickly yellow cast; they're exceptionally astringent.

HEART SALAD

This clever salad uses the hearts of both artichokes and palms, and beet slices cut into heart shapes with a cookie cutter. All in all, it's a Valentine wish for you and yours.

1	(14-oz.) can hearts of palm, drained and rinsed
1	(13¾-oz.) can hearts of artichokes (packed in water), drained, rinsed, and quartered
1	(15-oz.) can sliced beets, drained
1	tablespoon passion fruit syrup, or passion fruit drink concentrate*
2	teaspoons Champagne vinegar, or white wine vinegar
¼	teaspoon salt
¼	teaspoon freshly ground pepper
2	tablespoons almond or vegetable oil

6 servings.
Preparation time: 25 minutes.
Ready to serve: 25 minutes.

1 Cut hearts of palm into ½-inch pieces. If necessary, remove tough outer layer, leaving tender core. Mix in large bowl with artichoke hearts; mound in center of serving platter.

2 Using 1½-inch heart-shaped cookie cutter, cut each beet slice into small heart, discarding remainder. Use hearts to decorate platter, placing some on top of salad and some around it.

3 In small bowl, whisk passion fruit syrup, vinegar, salt and pepper until well combined. Whisk in oil in a slow, steady stream. Pour dressing over salad and serve at once.

TIP* Passion fruit syrup is a tangy concentrate, sometimes sold under the name "Condensed Passion Fruit Drink." It's available in Chinese and East Indian markets, and often used in marinades, dressings and fruity cocktails. For this salad, do not use canned passion fruit nectar, which is mixed with corn syrup and far too sweet.

O *rnamental votive holders add personality to your candlelit party. Micro beads are fun to use for decorating. Repeat the theme of the party onto the holders. Try a flower punch with jewel-tone beads for spring, or different leaf punches in earth-tone beads for fall.*

MATERIALS AND TOOLS

- ❏ VOTIVE CANDLE HOLDERS
- ❏ TEALIGHT CANDLES
- ❏ SHEET OF TACKY TAPE (WITH PAPER LINING)
- ❏ CLEAR MICRO BEADS
- ❏ SILVER MICRO BEADS
- ❏ SNOWFLAKE CRAFT PUNCH
- ❏ XACTO KNIFE (CRAFT KNIFE)

DIRECTIONS

1 Punch several snowflakes out of tacky tape (Tip: Use the handle punch accessory to ease punching through thicker paper, if necessary).

2 Peel off the paper backing and apply the snowflakes around the candle holder. Use an Xacto knife to help peel off the top piece of paper.

3 Pour a mix of clear and silver beads on top of each snowflake over a plate or bowl. If desired, brush a little clear-drying glue on clear tealight candle containers and shake glitter over them to add sparkle to your candles.

FORT CELERY

Lincoln grew up in a log cabin. Andrew Jackson, Benjamin Harrison, and Ulysses S. Grant all defended log forts. So we thought this salad fort would be the perfect tribute for your President's Day dinner. Why not have one of the kids read the Gettysburg Address before serving? To serve, remove the roof and scoop out the dressed salad. Make sure you remove all toothpicks and wooden spears when serving the fort itself.

2	large heads celery
12	(10-inch) bamboo skewers
10	cups mixed salad greens
⅔	cup purchased salad dressing, preferably ranch or a fruity vinaigrette
4	(5-inch) portobello mushrooms, cleaned
1	(8-oz.) can sliced water chestnuts

6 servings.
Preparation time: 1 hour.
Ready to serve: 1 hour.

1 Cut 16 (9-inch) celery ribs and 6 (4-inch) celery ribs. These will become the logs of the fort. To make the flags for the fort, reserve 4 inner flowery ribs.

2 To build walls of fort: On large serving platter or marble slab, use 4 (9-inch) ribs for each side. Overlap logs at the 90-degree corners, like a log building. Secure in place at the corners with bamboo skewer. Trim skewers so that ¼ inch sticks up above each corner.*

3 Cut two skewers so that they are long enough to pierce top log, run into the second log, yet stick up 4 inches over the top of the fort. Pierce these into place on opposite sides of the fort, then pull out (in effect, you've predrilled holes for the roof supports). Stick flowery flags onto skewers sticking up at each corner.

4 To build roof: Take 2 (4-inch) celery ribs and insert one of the short, pre-cut skewers into each, then run this skewer back into the pre-drilled holes, thereby creating a roof support on opposing walls of the fort. Lay 2 (4-inch) celery ribs 9 inches apart on your work surface; run three skewers through them, one at each end and one in the middle, thereby creating a roof frame. Repeat with remaining 4-inch ribs and three more skewers. Trim skewers on ends so that they're not sticking out of celery ribs. (You can make the fort up to this point 4 hours in advance; let stand at room temperature.)

5 Dress salad greens with purchased dressing. Place dressed greens inside fort. Pick up one roof frame and place it on one of the sides of the fort without a piece of celery sticking up from it. Lean the roof support against those two vertical celery stalks. Repeat with the second frame on the other side of the fort.

6 Slice mushrooms into ¼-inch slices; discard short end pieces. Lay long slices parallel to the celery ribs on the roof frames to form the roof's shingles.

7 Use sliced water chestnuts to form paving stones up to one side of the fort, like a path to the front door. Serve immediately.

TIP* Sturdy kitchen shears or wire cutters are best for cutting the bamboo skewers to the appropriate lengths.

VEALY GOOD STUFFED CABBAGE

Stuffed cabbage is definitely comfort food with a Jewish heritage, and perfect for a cold winter night. The meaty rolls are slowly simmered in a sweet-and-sour tomato sauce. Better yet, you can make ahead and reheat just before you're ready to serve them. Get the kids in on the act, teaching them how to roll the leaves into little bundles. If you can't find ground veal, use all ground beef.

1	lb. ground veal
½	lb. ground beef
¼	cup white rice (do not use instant rice)
1	small onion, minced
1	large garlic clove, minced
¼	cup chopped fresh parsley, washed
1	tablespoon chopped fresh dill or 2 teaspoons dried
½	teaspoon caraway seeds
2	teaspoons salt
½	teaspoon freshly ground pepper
1	large head savoy cabbage (about 2 lb.)
1	(28-oz.) can crushed tomatoes
1	(14.5-oz.) can chicken stock (regular or low-fat)
4	tablespoons cider vinegar
3	tablespoons raisins or dried currants
2	tablespoons packed brown sugar

6 servings.
Preparation time: 35 minutes.
Ready to serve: 2 hours, 10 minutes.

1 In large bowl, mix ground veal, ground beef, rice, onion, garlic, parsley, dill, caraway seeds, ½ teaspoon of the salt and pepper; combine gently but thoroughly. Do not mix until meats' fibers break down. Set aside while you prepare cabbage.

2 Prepare large bowl of ice water. Bring large pot of salted water and 1 teaspoon salt to a boil. Meanwhile, cut bottom core off cabbage and gently pull off leaves, taking care not to tear. Submerge cabbage leaves in boiling water, pressing down gently with wooden spoon; cook until flexible and tender, about 8 minutes. Drain, then gently submerge leaves in prepared ice water to stop cooking. Drain again; gently blot dry with paper towels.

3 Lay leaves on clean, dry work surface. Cut out thick center veins. Depending on how large leaf is, place as little as 2 tablespoons or as much as ¼ cup of the filling in center of leaf. Fold sides over stuffing. Roll leaf up, enclosing filling and folded-over sides. Place seam side down in large Dutch oven or large pot. Repeat with remaining leaves until all the stuffing is used. Discard remaining leaves, or reserve for another purpose.

4 Heat oven to 400°F. In large saucepan, bring tomatoes, chicken stock, vinegar, raisins, brown sugar, and remaining ½ teaspoon salt to a simmer over medium-high heat, stirring frequently. Pour over stuffed cabbage leaves in pot; cover and bake 1 hour. Uncover and baste; bake an additional 30 minutes, basting every 5 minutes. Remove from oven; cover and let stand 5 minutes, then serve.

Ossobuco with Wild Mushrooms

This may be the very definition of Italian comfort food: veal shanks, slow-roasted with aromatic vegetables and herbs, the marrow slowly melting and thickening the sauce as the bones bake. What a dinner on a cold holiday night! If you're having lots of company, double the recipe and make two pots' worth.

3	tablespoons olive oil
6	(¾-lb.) veal shanks, trimmed of any excess fat
1	large onion, minced
3	medium carrots, thinly sliced
3	ribs celery, thinly sliced
2	large garlic cloves, minced
½	lb. wild mushrooms, such as cremini, porcini, or a mixture, cleaned and halved
1	cup dry vermouth or white wine
1	cup chicken stock
1	(14-oz.) can diced tomatoes (with their juice)
1	teaspoon dried thyme or 2 teaspoons fresh thyme
2	teaspoons chopped fresh rosemary or 1 teaspoon dried, crumbled
1	teaspoon lemon peel
2	bay leaves
½	teaspoon salt, or to taste
½	teaspoon freshly ground pepper
2	tablespoons tomato paste

Serves 6.
Preparation time: 12 minutes.
Ready to serve: 2 hours, 30 minutes.

1 Heat oven to 350°F. In Dutch oven, heat 1½ tablespoons of the oil over medium-high heat until hot. Add veal shanks, in batches if necessary; brown all sides, turning occasionally, about 5 minutes. Transfer to plates.

2 Add remaining 1½ tablespoons oil to Dutch over. Stir in onion, carrots, celery, and garlic; cook, stirring frequently, until softened, about 3 minutes. Add mushrooms; cook 5 minutes or until they release their liquid and it evaporates to a glaze. Stir in wine, scraping up browned bits on bottom. Stir in stock, diced tomatoes, thyme, rosemary, lemon peel, and bay leaves. Return shanks and any juices to Dutch oven, nestling into sauce.

3 Bake, covered, 2 hours, or until meat is falling off bones. If shanks are not all submerged in liquid, gently move them around every 30 minutes to steep in sauce.

4 Remove from oven; set over medium heat. Stir in tomato paste. Season with salt and pepper; simmer 5 minutes or until tomato paste thickens sauce. Remove and discard bay leaves. Serve at once.

ROLLED SOLE

Here's an entree the kids can help with. Once you've sautéed the vegetables for the filling, they can roll the delicate sole fillets around the cheesy stuffing. Use only fresh herbs — the cooking is too quick to soften dried herbs. To mellow the flavors further, refrigerate the rolls 2 hours before baking.

3	tablespoons olive oil
1	medium onion, minced
1	large garlic clove, minced
2	tablespoons chopped toasted almonds
2	tablespoons chopped fresh parsley
2	tablespoons chopped fresh dill
2	teaspoons grated lemon peel
5	oz. feta cheese, crumbled
6	(4-oz.) sole fillets
½	teaspoon salt
½	teaspoon freshly ground pepper
¾	teaspoon mild or hot paprika*

6 servings.
Preparation time: 15 minutes.
Ready to serve: 35 minutes.

1 Heat oven to 400°F. In large skillet, heat 1 tablespoons olive oil over medium heat until hot. Add onion and garlic; cook 2 minutes, stirring frequently until softened. Stir in almonds, parsley, dill, and lemon peel. Remove pan from heat; stir in feta.

2 Lay fillets on clean, dry work surface; season each with salt and pepper. Spread 2 tablespoons filling on each fillet. Roll gently away from you. Rub each roll with ½ teaspoon olive oil. Place seam side down in shallow baking dish. Season each with ⅛ teaspoon paprika.

3 Bake 12 minutes, or until filling is bubbling and fish is cooked through. Let stand 5 minutes at room temperature before serving.

TIP* The chile oils in paprika (simply a type of red peppers, powdered) break down very quickly. It then is no longer a piquant spice but the familiar coloring agent on your grandmother's deviled eggs. You can try to revitalize stale paprika by toasting it in a dry skillet over low heat 2 minutes, or until aromatic. Hot paprika (sometimes labeled "Hot Hungarian Paprika") is equivalent in heat to cayenne pepper.

OVEN BARBECUED BRISKET

Texas has given us barbecued brisket — a luscious way to make this inexpensive cut of meat tender and juicy, even in winter when the barbecue grill is on hiatus. Barbecuing in the oven makes for an even easier technique, and this recipe fills the house with wonderful aromas as it slow-cooks. Use your favorite barbecue sauce. You'll have to start the night before, but you'll end up with a roast so tender, no one can turn it down.

1	(5-lb.) beef brisket, trimmed
1	teaspoon onion salt
1	teaspoon freshly ground pepper
½	teaspoon garlic powder
1	tablespoon liquid smoke
2	tablespoons Worcestershire sauce
2	cups purchased barbecue sauce

6 servings.
Preparation time: 10 minutes.
Ready to serve: 16 hours, 40 minutes.

1 The night before, line 13x9-inch baking pan with aluminum foil; lay brisket on top. Massage onion salt, pepper and garlic powder into meat, then drizzle on liquid smoke. Seal foil tightly, creating a packet; refrigerate at least 8 hours or up to 24 hours.

2 The next morning, open packet and drizzle Worcestershire sauce over meat. Seal again and refrigerate at least 4 hours or up to 12 hours.

3 Heat oven to 350°F. Place sealed packet into prepared pan; bake 4½ hours.

4 Open foil and pour barbecue sauce onto meat. Bake, uncovered, 30 minutes or until fork tender.

5 Remove brisket from sauce; let stand 10 minutes before carving. Meanwhile, drain sauce in pan; deglaze. Slice brisket against the grain, passing sauce alongside.

HERB ROASTED GAME HENS

By the time New Year's Day rolls around, we're all sick of turkey. So why make another?
Flavorful, herb-crusted, game hens bake up moist and light every time.

6	(1-lb) medium game hens, giblets and necks removed
½	cup olive oil
2	tablespoons chopped fresh rosemary
2	tablespoons chopped fresh parsley
1	tablespoon fresh thyme
½	teaspoon onion salt
½	teaspoon freshly ground pepper
¼	teaspoon garlic powder
1	teaspoon minced dried rosemary, or 2 teaspoons minced fresh rosemary
1	rib celery, finely chopped
1	medium scallion, green part only, finely chopped

6 servings.
Preparation time: 20 minutes.
Ready to serve: 1 hour, 10 minutes.

1 Heat oven to 375°F. Rinse game hens and pat dry. In blender or food processor fitted with chopping blade, or blender, combine olive oil, rosemary, parsley, thyme, onion salt, pepper and garlic powder; pulse 4 or 5 times to create paste, scraping down sides of bowl as necessary. Rub paste onto hens, spreading evenly onto breast meat and legs.

2 Combine celery and scallion; place 1 tablespoon (or more) in each body cavity.

3 Place birds in large baking dish; bake 30 minutes. Bake an additional 15 minutes or until cooked through and juices from thigh run clear, basting with pan juices every 5 minutes. A meat thermometer inserted into thickest part of thigh should register 160°F. Let stand at room temperature 5 minutes. Remove celery and scallions from insides, then serve.

INDOOR BLOOMING NARCISSUS

Blooming flowers make beautiful decorations in the home during the dormant winter. These paperwhites make a cheerful centerpiece at the dinner table. The frosted white sea glass complements a winter themed party. Try growing amaryllis bulbs in potted soil for a different variety of forced-blooming flower.

MATERIALS AND TOOLS

❏ PAPERWHITE BULBS (FROM LOCAL NURSERY)
❏ GLASS CONTAINER
❏ SEA GLASS

DIRECTIONS

1 Fill the container about 1½ inches full of sea glass, allowing room for root growth.

2 Place several bulbs in the container. Make sure they are not touching each other or the sides of the container.

3 Fill the container with more sea glass, covering two-thirds of the bulbs. Fill with water, but only enough to barely touch the bottoms of the bulbs. Do not allow the bulbs to sit in water because they will become moldy. Place in a cool sunny spot. Blooms in about 3 to 4 weeks.

PINE NUT RICE PILAF

Here's the perfect side for ossobuco or most any dish: A light, nutty pilaf. Sweet and aromatic, pine nuts come from the piñon tree, common in the American Southwest as well as Italy. Because of their high fat content, they unfortunately turn rancid quickly. Freeze in sealed plastic bags for up to 1 year; always check to make sure they smell fresh like pine trees, not tangy or dusty.

2	tablespoons pine nuts
2	tablespoons canola oil or other vegetable oil
1	medium onion, minced
1	teaspoon finely grated lemon peel
¼	teaspoon grated nutmeg
1¼	cups white rice
2½	cups chicken stock or vegetable stock (regular, low-fat or nonfat)
¼	teaspoon salt, or to taste
¼	teaspoon freshly ground pepper

6 servings.
Preparation time: 7 minutes.
Ready to serve: 35 minutes.

1 In small skillet, toast nuts over medium heat until lightly browned, about 3 minutes, stirring often. Set aside.

2 In medium saucepan, heat oil over medium heat until hot. Add onion; sauté until softened, about 3 minutes. Stir in lemon peel and nutmeg. Add rice; cook 10 seconds, stirring constantly. Pour in stock and stir in toasted nuts.

3 Bring mixture to a simmer; cover and reduce heat to low. Cook 15 minutes or until rice is tender. Remove from heat; let stand, covered, 5 minutes. Season with salt and pepper; fluff with fork and serve.

BLACK-EYED PEAS WITH BACON AND ESCAROLE

In many parts of the South, black-eyed peas are traditional New Year's fare. They're said to signal good luck for the year ahead, but it's actually something of a mistake. It wasn't the peas that were the good luck; it was the greens tucked into them. The greens were said to symbolize money in the new year. Here we've used escarole, a member of the endive family and popular in Italian cooking. It's sweet and tender, giving the peas a delicate richness without a lot of added fat.

3	tablespoons canola or other vegetable oil
9	thick slices bacon, roughly chopped
3	garlic cloves, thinly sliced
2	small heads escarole (about 8 oz. each), cored, broken into leaves, washed but not dried, and chopped into 1-inch strips
2	(15-oz.) cans black-eyed peas, drained and rinsed
½	cup chopped fresh parsley
½	teaspoon freshly ground pepper
3	dashes hot pepper sauce, or to taste
⅛	teaspoon salt

6 servings.
Preparation time: 10 minutes.
Ready to serve: 25 minutes.

1 In large saucepan, heat oil over medium heat until hot. Add bacon and garlic; cook until bacon is frizzled at edges, about 4 minutes, stirring frequently.

2 Add escarole; toss well. Cover pan and cook until escarole is wilted, about 2 minutes. Stir in beans, parsley and pepper. Cover and reduce heat to medium-low; cook 10 minutes, stirring once in a while.

3 Stir in pepper and hot pepper sauce. Season with salt, if desired. Serve immediately.

CAJUN POMMES FRITES

In honor of the Louisiana Purchase, Mr. Jefferson's most lavish shopping spree, serve up these crunchy french fries, doused with Cajun spices. The trick to crisp fries is to fry them twice: once at a low temperature, then again at a high temperature. Season them the moment they're out of the fryer the second time.

6	Russet potatoes, scrubbed
	Vegetable oil for frying
½	teaspoon salt
½	teaspoon dried thyme
¼	teaspoon dried basil, crumbled
¼	teaspoon onion powder
¼	teaspoon garlic powder
¼	teaspoon freshly ground black pepper
⅛	teaspoon cayenne pepper, or to taste

6 servings.
Preparation time: 20 minutes.
Ready to serve: 45 minutes.

1 Fill large bowl with water. Peel potatoes; cut into ¼-inch-thick strips. Alternatively, peel potatoes and cut into fries using mandoline with french-fry blade, or food processor filled with french-fry blade. Soak strips in water 5 minutes to leach excess starch.

2 Clip deep-frying thermometer to inside of large pot; heat oil over medium-high heat to 250°F. Drain potatoes; pat dry with paper towels. Fry potatoes until golden, about 4 minutes, working in batches as necessary. Do not crowd pan; adjust heat to maintain temperature. Alternatively, place oil in deep fryer and heat to 250°F according to manufacturer's instructions; fry as directed above. Transfer fries to cookie sheets or plates lined with paper towels; drain and let cool to room temperature. The recipe can be made to this point up to 5 hours in advance; let fries stand at room temperature. Do not drain oil from pot or deep fryer.

3 Meanwhile, in small bowl, mix salt, thyme, basil, onion powder, garlic powder, pepper and cayenne; set aside.

4 Reheat oil to 360°F. Fry potatoes until deep golden brown, about 3 minutes, working in batches as necessary and adjusting temperature to maintain heat. Transfer to plates lined with paper towels to drain; season with spice mixture the moment fries come out of the oil. Serve immediately.

ROASTED TOMATOES AND SHALLOTS

At high heat, these shallots caramelize into a sweet, garlicky delight, the perfect foil to tomatoes — and to cheese-filled Rolled Sole *(page 162). Around Valentine's Day, tomatoes aren't at their best, so this recipe uses cherry tomatoes, which can stand up to long shipping and thus arrive in our markets from Chile and parts south in better condition than larger tomatoes.*

6	medium shallots, peeled and quartered*
¼	cup olive oil
½	teaspoon salt
½	teaspoon freshly ground pepper
30	cherry tomatoes (about 1½ lb.)

6 servings.
Preparation time: 5 minutes.
Ready to serve: 30 minutes.

1 Heat oven to 400°F. In 13x9-inch baking pan, toss shallots, oil, salt and pepper; bake until shallots are soft and aromatic, about 25 minutes, stirring once or twice.

2 Add tomatoes to prepared pan; toss to coat. Bake until tomatoes crack at skin, about 15 additional minutes, stirring occasionally. Let stand at room temperature 5 minutes before serving.

TIP* Keep the root end attached to the shallots after you've peeled them. That way, the quarters will stay intact as they're roasted in the pan.

This snow-and-icicle-inspired lamp shade will add a whimsical touch to your winter holiday table. Table lamps create the feeling of an intimate atmosphere. Try painting the shade before applying glitter, to create any color lamp shade you desire.

DIRECTIONS

1 Briskly brush clear acrylic medium onto the lamp shade (it dries fairly quickly).

2 Pour glitter over the shade. After it has dried, spray it with clear acrylic sealant.

3 Attach double-stick tape to the trim. Peel the paper back and attach the trim underneath the bottom of the lamp shade. Cut the excess off. Spray-painting the base white is optional.

WINE BRAISED RADISHES

It's high time radishes got off the relish tray. Cooked, they're sweet and peppery, a delightful side dish. Look for radishes still attached to their greens — this is an assurance that they're fresh, that they haven't been stored for months in plastic bags. Wash them carefully to remove any grit. If serving these with a Hanukkah meal, use margarine, not butter, to retain the kosher ethic of the meal.

2	tablespoons margarine or butter
30	large radishes, preferably of multiple colors
½	teaspoon salt
¼	teaspoon freshly ground pepper
½	cup red wine (American Cabernet Sauvignon or French Côte-du-Rhône)

6 servings.
Preparation time: 10 minutes.
Ready to serve: 35 minutes.

1 In large skillet or sauté pan, melt margarine over low heat. Add radishes; cook 5 minutes, stirring frequently.

2 Sprinkle with salt and pepper. Increase heat to medium-high; pour in wine, scraping up any browned bits on bottom. Bring to a simmer; cover and reduce heat to low. Simmer until radishes are tender but still crisp, about 15 minutes.

3 Transfer radishes from pan to serving bowl; tent with aluminum foil to keep warm. Increase heat to high; boil down liquid until reduced to a glaze, about 3 minutes. Pour over radishes and serve.

WHITE CHOCOLATE STRAWBERRY CUPS

These easy chocolate cups are the perfect end to a Valentine's Day dinner. Foil candy cups are available from any candy supplier. These chocolate treats are romantic and very sweet. And best of all, since chocolate melts at body temperature, your kids can work with it once you've melted it, and there will be no fear they'll get burned.

6	tablespoons white chocolate chips, or 6 tablespoons finely chopped white chocolate*
12	foil candy cups (1-inch wide by ¾-inch high)
3	tablespoons strawberry jam (not strawberry preserves)

6 servings.
Preparation time: 40 minutes.
Ready to serve: 3 hours, 40 minutes.

1 Place white chocolate in small microwavable bowl; microwave on High 1 minute or until nearly melted; remove bowl from microwave and stir chocolate until smooth.

2 Spoon ¾ teaspoon melted chocolate into one foil cup. Using small flat paintbrush, spread evenly over bottom and sides. Repeat with remaining cups. Arrange on plate; refrigerate until firm, about 4 minutes.

3 Spoon ¾ teaspoon jam into each chocolate-lined cup. Tap on counter to settle jam. Reheat remaining chocolate in microwave on High 15 seconds; stir until smooth. Spoon ½ teaspoon melted chocolate over top of jam in each cup; use brush to spread chocolate to sides so it seals in the jam.

4 Refrigerate until firm, about 4 minutes, or allow chocolate to firm up at room temperature, about 3 hours.

TIP* Since white chocolate is all cocoa butter and sugar, but without any cocoa solids, it melts perfectly in the microwave, as in this recipe. If you prefer, you can put it in the top half of a double boiler and melt over simmering water, stirring constantly. Let cool 5 minutes before proceeding with the recipe.

RASPBERRY NUT CAKE

Nut cake is traditionally served at Passover. The ground nuts stand in for the flour, missing from a kosher house during those 8 days. Here, the cake's reinvented for Hanukkah. There's a little flour for body, but the egg whites give it a soufflé-like texture. All in all, it's a surprisingly light ending to a traditional Hanukkah — or any holiday — meal.

1¼	ups sliced almonds
6	tablespoons chopped pecan pieces
6	tablespoons chopped walnut pieces
¾	cup granulated sugar
¼	cup packed light brown sugar
4	large egg yolks, at room temperature
½	teaspoon ground cinnamon
¼	teaspoon salt
2	teaspoons vanilla extract
3	tablespoons almond, walnut oil or canola oil
2	teaspoons all-purpose flour
8	large egg whites, beaten stiff
	Nonstick cooking spray
1	cup raspberry jam
1½	tablespoons confectioners' sugar
	Fresh raspberries, for garnish
	Fresh mint, for garnish

6 servings.
Preparation time: 30 minutes.
Ready to serve: 3 hours, 30 minutes.

1 Heat oven to 350°F. Toast nuts on large lipped baking sheet until lightly browned, about 4 minutes, stirring frequently. Let cool 10 minutes. Transfer to food processor fitted with chopping blade; pulse just until ground, not until paste-like. Alternatively, work in batches in mortar with pestle. Set ground nuts aside; maintain oven temperature.

2 In large bowl, beat granulated sugar, brown sugar, egg yolks, cinnamon and salt with electric mixer at medium speed until pale and thick, about 3 minutes. Beat in vanilla, then oil, flour and ground nuts. Continue beating until thoroughly incorporated.

3 Using rubber spatula, stir in ⅓ of the beaten egg whites. The batter will be quite stiff. Mix until no egg whites are visible. Fold in half of the remaining egg whites until incorporated. Then very gently fold in remaining egg whites just until evenly distributed through the batter — there will be some white streaks.

4 Spray 8-inch springform pan with nonstick cooking spray. Gently spoon batter into pan, taking care not to lose height of egg whites. Bake 40 minutes or until slightly puffed and browned. The cake may feel slightly unset in the middle; because of so many egg whites, a cake tester will not work. Cool on wire rack to room temperature — the cake will shrink away from the sides of the pan as it cools.

5 In small bowl, soften jam in microwave on High 1 minute. Unmold from pan. Gently slice cake in two horizontally, creating two layers. Carefully remove top layer with wide spatula. Spread bottom layer with jam. Replace top layer. Sprinkle with confectioners' sugar and serve. Or, store tightly covered, at room temperature, up to 2 days. Garnish with fresh raspberries and mint.

MENDIANT

This traditional French bark is a wonderful pleasure, a beautiful treat at the end of a celebratory meal. Mendiant means "beggar" in French — probably indicative of what your guests will do when they see this dessert coming to the table. For an even more decadent delight, take 2 (3-inch) squares of edible gold leaf, available from candy suppliers, and dab it or blow it over the Mendiant once it's completely cooled. Traditionally made with dark chocolate, you can substitute milk chocolate if you prefer. Serve with strong coffee or tea.

12	oz. bittersweet or dark chocolate, chopped
¼	cup shelled salted pistachios
¼	cup dried cranberries, or dried cherries, or dried blueberries
2	tablespoons chopped crystallized ginger

6 servings.
Preparation time: 10 minutes.
Ready to serve: 4 hours, 30 minutes.

1 Line large cookie sheet with silicon baking mat, or sprinkle a few drops of water on cookie sheet and line with parchment paper.

2 Place chocolate in top of double boiler set over simmering water. If you don't have a double boiler, place chocolate in heat-safe bowl that fits snugly over a small pot of simmering water. Stir constantly until half of the chocolate is melted. Remove top part of double boiler or bowl from pot, then continue stirring off the heat until chocolate is completely melted. Cool 5 minutes. Alternatively, melt chocolate by placing in large bowl; microwave on High 1 minute, stir well, then microwave an additional 2 minutes or until half the chocolate is melted. Remove from microwave and continue stirring until chocolate is fully melted. Ideally, you can use a chocolate thermometer and never let the mixture get hotter than 110°F, then quickly stir it until it's 90°F. Although this is a step preferred among professional candy-makers, it is not necessary unless you intend to store the Mendiant for more than 1 day.

3 Pour melted chocolate onto the prepared cookie sheet; spread to ⅛ inch thickness using offset spatula or rubber spatula. Sprinkle fruit and nuts evenly over top of chocolate. Gently press into chocolate with back of clean wooden spoon (clean, so as not to get chocolate on the fruit and nuts). Do not press down deeply; just make sure they adhere. Let stand at room temperature at least 4 hours to firm up, or place in refrigerator for no more than 30 minutes, just to set chocolate. Break into pieces to serve.

ZUPPE INGLESI

There's no more classic Italian cake than this — named an "English soup" because of the pastry cream that separates the spongy génoise layers. Store this cake tightly covered in the refrigerator — that way, the whipped cream will not pick up food odors.

CAKE

1	cup plus 2 tablespoons cake flour
1½	teaspoons baking powder
¼	teaspoon salt
5	large eggs, separated
1	cup plus 2 tablespoons sugar
3	tablespoons milk (regular, low-fat or nonfat)
½	teaspoon vanilla extract
½	teaspoon almond extract

PASTRY CREAM

¾	cup sugar
6	tablespoons all-purpose flour
½	teaspoon salt
3	cups milk (regular, low-fat or nonfat)
6	large egg yolks, lightly beaten
2	teaspoons vanilla extract
1	cup chopped candied fruit

TOPPING

1	cup rum
4	cups heavy cream
3	tablespoons confectioners' sugar
	Additional pieces chopped candied fruit for garnish

10 servings.
Preparation time: 20 minutes.
Ready to serve: 4 hours, 30 minutes.

1 Position rack in center of oven; heat oven to 375°F. Cover 12x16-inch jelly-roll pan with parchment paper; set aside.

2 For Cake: In medium bowl, sift flour, baking powder and salt; set aside. In large bowl, beat egg whites with electric mixer at high speed until frothy.* Beat in ½ cup sugar in slow, thin stream until soft peaks form, scraping down bowl's sides as necessary. Set aside.

3 Clean and dry beaters. In another large bowl, beat yolks with electric mixer at medium speed until thick. Add ½ cup plus 2 tablespoons sugar; continue beating until pale yellow and fluffy, about 3 minutes. Beat in milk, vanilla extract, and almond extract. Using rubber spatula, fold in sifted flour mixture, then gently fold in egg whites, taking care not to press down or beat. Gently spread batter into prepared jelly-roll pan.

4 Bake about 18 minutes or until golden brown. Cool on wire rack in pan 10 minutes, then cover rack with parchment paper and invert pan onto wire rack. Remove parchment paper that was on bottom of cake and cool cake to room temperature. Trim off edges; cut into three equal, rectangular pieces to become the Zuppe Inglesi's layers.

5 For Pastry Cream: In medium saucepan, whisk sugar, flour, salt and milk over medium heat until simmering. Cook 1 minute, then whisk ½ cup of this mixture into beaten egg yolks until smooth. Whisk egg-yolk mixture back into saucepan, set over very low heat, and cook 30 seconds, or until slightly thickened and mixture coats back of wooden spoon, stirring constantly. Remove from heat; whisk in candied fruit and vanilla. Pour into clean, large bowl. Place plastic wrap directly on surface to prevent skin from forming on custard and cool to room temperature. (You can make the pastry cream in advance. Store, covered with plastic wrap, in the refrigerator for up to 1 day.)

6 To build cake: Sprinkle top of each layer with ⅓ cup rum, dipping pastry brush into rum and dabbing it onto cake. Do not brush so as not to tear cake. Place one layer on serving plate; spread with half of prepared pastry cream. Lay second cake layer on cream, then spread with remaining pastry cream. Top with third cake layer.

7 For Topping: Using chilled, clean beaters and a chilled, large bowl, beat heavy cream with electric mixer at high speed until frothy. Beat in sugar in slow, steady stream until cream is smooth and somewhat stiff. Do not beat until dry or buttery.

Spread whipped cream over cake, or pipe it over cake using pastry bag fitted with #8 star tip. To decorate, drop candied fruit pieces over top of cake. Store in refrigerator.

TIP* To get the best height out of the egg whites, make sure that they're at room temperature, that the bowl is completely dry, and that there's not one spot of yolk in the whites.

CHOCOLATE CHERRY TURNOVERS

To celebrate George Washington's vaunted honesty, we've recreated those cherry turnovers so popular from our childhoods, crossing them with that French delight pains au chocolat, *or chocolate croissants. Any way you serve them, with or without ice cream, for dessert or breakfast, your family will surely tell you they love these — and they too won't be lying!*

1	(15-oz.) can Bing cherries in syrup, drained and roughly chopped
6	tablespoons semisweet or bittersweet chocolate chips
¼	teaspoon corn starch
1	(17.3-oz.) pkg. frozen puff pastry, thawed according to the package's instructions
	All-purpose flour for dusting work surface
1	large egg, at room temperature, beaten with 1 tablespoon water
¾	teaspoon sugar

6 servings.
Preparation time: 25 minutes.
Ready to serve: 50 minutes.

1 In medium bowl, mix cherries, chocolate chips and corn starch; set aside. Heat oven to 400°F.

2 Unfold puff pastry sheets onto lightly dusted, dry work surface. Roll each sheet to 12-inch square. Cut into quarters. Reserve two quarters for another use.

3 Place 2 tablespoons cherry mixture in square, shaping it into small log that runs from one corner to opposite corner. Brush two adjacent sides of square with egg mixture, then fold two dry sides over filling to meet moistened sides. Press to seal; use fork to crimp closed. Brush top with egg mixture; sprinkle with ⅛ teaspoon sugar. Arrange on baking sheet. Repeat with remaining squares.

4 Bake until golden brown, about 20 minutes. Cool on wire rack 5 minutes before serving.

Red roses are a classic symbol of love. Ivy symbolizes fidelity and friendship. Inspired by Valentine's Day, this romantic centerpiece celebrates the beauty of love. Create this candlelit floral centerpiece using a variety of flowers to fit your occasion.

MATERIALS AND TOOLS

- ❏ CANDLE HOLDER WITH SIDES
- ❏ ROSES
- ❏ IVY
- ❏ CLUB CANDLE
- ❏ FLORAL CAKE FOAM
- ❏ UTILITY SHEARS
- ❏ KNIFE

DIRECTIONS

1 Press the top of the candle holder onto the foam to make an impression which you will use to carve along. Cut around the foam to fit the diameter of the candle holder. Slice the foam to a desired height. Cut around the top of the foam to create a rounded top.

2 Soak the floral foam in tepid water about 10 minutes until fully saturated. Place the foam on top of the candle holder and insert the candle in the center of the foam.

3 Arrange cut roses into the foam. Fill with cut ivy and insert longer vines near the bottom.